How to Satisfy Your Woman

The complete and uncensored sex guide

Larry Lewitan

Copyright © Larry A. Lewitan, 2010

Larry A. Lewitan asserts the moral right
to be identified as the author of this work.

All rights reserved. No part of this publication may be reproduced, stored in or introduced into a retrieval system, or transmitted, in any form or my any means, electronic, mechanical, photocopying, recording or otherwise, without the prior written permission of the copyright owner.

ISBN 978-965-91612-1-8

To the woman I love,

to the woman that believed,

And

to all the women and men that have better sex after reading this book.

CONTENTS

Preface *3*
On your marks, get sex, go! *4*
Why is sex so fucking important? *7*
Choose your pussy wisely *13*
Is fucking a skill you can learn? *18*
Is your dick tuned in to the right channel? *23*
Listen to the pussy! *30*
The fucking code *38*
Fountain of joy *56*
King of the castle *64*
Come outside *76*
Push-ups, Sit-ups, Sex-up *93*
Foreplay vs. Foul play *96*
The truth about porn *117*
Enjoy the toy *130*
Backdoor to heaven *143*
Dress up, sex up *149*
Sexcuses *158*
Shrink it *170*

How to Satisfy Your Woman

PREFACE

Why are most women unhappy with their man's performance in bed? Why do most men not have a clue how to sexually satisfy their woman?

The author maintains that sexual unhappiness in a relationship is caused by the man's lack of experience, knowledge and understanding when it comes to satisfying his woman. He also maintains that sex is the most important pillar in a relationship, and that without good sex no relationship can survive!

These are strong statements, and the book offers powerful solutions by going to the root cause of sexual unhappiness among couples. Written in explicit, uninhibited language, the kind that men can understand, this is an uncensored guidebook that instructs men on how to satisfy their woman. It holds nothing back. The sexual techniques that it details, as well as the wisdom that it presents, will allow men to be able to fuck their woman the way she dreams of being fucked.

Women will read it too. They'll enjoy the tongue-in-cheek humor and be thrilled that one of the world's best kept secrets (how to make love to a woman) is finally coming out of the closet. If their men don't buy this book, it's certain they'll be buying it for them.

ON YOUR MARKS, GET SEX, GO!

Is sex the most important aspect of a successful relationship? Hell yeah, for sure. This is my standpoint and I will justify it by approaching this subject from various angles – mostly from the viewpoint of men. The purpose of this book is to provide a down-to-earth assessment of how to please your woman by understanding the underlying forces that make a relationship successful and tying everything back to the fundamental structure that supports a long lasting, fulfilling and loving relationship – sex.

Many books have been written and documentaries filmed on this subject, a fact that underscores the importance of sex in our daily lives. I take it a step further by proclaiming that it is the most important building block in our lives because we, as men are naturally programmed to strive to satisfy our sexual desires. Relationships with women are complex and require us to be creative if we want to avoid the daily pitfalls that deny us our sexual gratification. In particular, we must learn to control our high testosterone levels that define us as men but make us emotionally insensitive to picking up female needs and addressing them appropriately.

I tackle this subject by using a language that we men understand – profane, dirty, and yes, to some it might seem disrespectful or insulting towards women, but let me assure you that this is not my intention. I believe that by using the standard language that we men can relate to, I am able to get my point across better, and that is the main purpose of this book. Therefore, if any women read this (and I hope you will), please don't take my objectification of the female personally. I love women and appreciate everything about them. I even go so far as to admit that I am obsessed with understanding them, so I can better please them. Even when I was a boy, I was driven by my sexual desires to understand the subject of sex, and as I got older, to excel at the art of sex. Yes, my fellow men, fucking is a true art and we as men need to embrace this as a fact of life.

I am not going to bore you with studies, reports, statistics or medical findings. You will not hear from me any psychological chit chat on how to unravel the psyche of women or how to think like they do in the hope of better understanding why a pussy is different from a dick. I also don't want to bore you with a lot of statistics – only one: **studies claim that up to 76% of women are disappointed with their male partner's performance in bed.**

WE ARE HERE TO CHANGE THAT!

What you will find on the following pages are the raw and basic principles of how a man and woman can have great sex. My advice is the result of a keen sense of observation, an ability to sense the slightest nuances in the physical and emotional language of women, the fact that I have always been fascinated with the art of sex, and the fact that I am strongly in tune with my feminine side (please…I am not referring to being gay – just in case some of you guys don't get it).

I am going to pour my heart out to you on this subject, and if I am able to educate you and to convince some of you about what I believe is necessary to get your woman to crave your dick, then I know I will have attained my goal in writing this book. Having said that, I ask you to keep an open mind when reading through these pages and to find the time to contemplate what you might learn. You may be appalled or in disagreement with some of my views, but there is a lot of common sense and experience mixed into my sexual philosophy, and if you are able to take a step back and free your mind from the sexual constraints laid on you by society, your education and your upbringing, then I am certain it will provide you with a refreshing and unleashing point of view.

WHY IS SEX SO FUCKING IMPORTANT?

Hello!!! Just the mere fact that I have to elaborate on this question means that some of you are oblivious to what's happening all around you. Yes, of course, sex is still more important to us men then to women (or so it seems), but this doesn't imply that women don't seek a great fuck; they just have a different definition of a great fuck and I am about to shed some light on their point of view.

So before we dive into the hands-on advice about how to please our women, let's first set the stage to understand the underlying forces that influence our sexual appetites.

First of all, embrace the fact that you are a cock-driven creature, and that everything you do is, to some extent, an extension of you sexual desire, or at least influenced by it. Your dick is nothing but the needle on a compass and north points to the pussy. So when we are sexually out of balance, we tend to act wrongly and this affects many of our daily decisions. Think of it this way – your dick is a pressure valve to release your tensions, and if you don't clean the hose regularly, the mounting pressure will erupt in unexpected ways. You're at the mercy of your hormones – or your dick for that matter. Not without reason there is a saying that warns: "Don't think with your dick".

Therefore, we men have to make sure our sexual appetite is satisfied at all times and that we do not starve our most important inner desire – a situation that can lead to sexual malnutrition. Now, this is not often easily achievable, even for men with a woman at their side, and here arises the problem we have to face head on. How do we get our women to fuck more often…and really enjoy it, so that they want to keep fucking us whenever we are in the mood for sex – because we are typically more in the mood for it than they are.

Of course many men seek the path of least resistance, which is to give up and seek alternative ways to satisfy the urge: an easy co-worker, an unsatisfied woman they happen to meet, or a professional hooker are some typical options that jump to mind. Yes, these are easy ways to get our daily fix. For a man, fucking is comparable to any form of addictive behavior where the addict is looking for his next endorphin kick. Once the urge overcomes us, we will do almost anything to stick our dick into a welcoming pussy (or mouth if a blow job is your thing), but the ramifications are far reaching. If you have deep pockets, you may choose to enjoy the short-lived experience with a strange and hopefully disease-free woman. Otherwise, like with every other addiction, you will have to revert to a less expensive drug to get your fix – in other words, porn.

What would the world be without porn – the inexpensive and safe way to jack off and release the tension? But more about porn – and its important contribution to men's sexual balance or imbalance – in a later chapter.

I am not going to judge anyone on what he believes he has to do to get his daily fix. However, did you ever stop and think that maybe, just maybe, we men have to work a little harder for the affection of our woman? We need to try to figure out what it is we want from our woman and then figure out what she needs from us. It's about reaching a mutual understanding so that in the end our needs will be satisfied and so will hers.

Not easy, but definitely doable, and I can promise you that once the two of you reach common ground, your urges will be satisfied, at least to the point where it will keep you from chasing after every skirt in town. For sure it will get you to think twice about whether sticking your dick into another woman is worth endangering your current relationship.

So before you go around and succumb to your craving for pussy, ass or tits – whatever your preference is – you should take a deep breath, suppress your animal instincts for a moment, and think. It is often that these extra few seconds that are decisive in determining the route of action we take. Without these extra seconds, we are just animals acting on our raw instincts and urges. But we are better than that – at least most of us are. Looking at a nicely formed ass, or at the crotch of a woman fitted into a pair of tight jeans, or glimpsing a pair of nice tits stuffed into a too tight t-shirt, or gasping at a perfectly formed cleavage staring back at you, is just healthy behavior – it just confirms that you are a man and that everything works as nature intended. It is true that we men are very susceptible and unconsciously drawn to these types of sexual signals, but please know that women know this as well and they secretly seek the attention. Every woman wants to be desired and most of them will go to extra lengths to ensure they receive the occasional stare, but it doesn't mean they want to be constantly stared at or grabbed at, or be addressed in an untactful manner (some men do actually think that foul language appeals to women – that's just ridiculous!).

Men need to understand that women are conflicted creatures – I hate generalizing, so for the record please note that I always refer to most women. On the one hand, they are not announcing that they are ready to jump into bed with every man coming their way, but they love the extra attention and knowing that men are fantasizing about them. For most women getting the extra attention is more than enough to satisfy their needs.

Look at this from a different angle: wouldn't it be disturbing to know that women were as dick-driven as we are pussy-driven? Promiscuity would rule the world, not that we don't have enough of that going on already, but the world would be one huge whore house and all our social values would deteriorate and eventually evaporate. So it's a good thing that it's hard to conquer our women. It would be intolerable to men if women were easy creatures, ready to suck off every dick in their reach. They are supposed to embody the better values that we men lack. They take care of our kids, they take on motherly tasks that we are incapable of, and they provide us with a warm bed, comfort and a sense of security – at least most of the time. Our society still quietly accepts the cliché that men cannot be faithful (although I vehemently oppose this) and that women that follow in the footsteps of men and indulge in sexual escapades are nothing but whores. Well, well, it's time to change that attitude wouldn't you say?

If a woman goes out to find some dick, this can only mean she isn't getting any, she isn't getting enough, or the dick is fucking her the wrong way (don't take it personally). Any one of these options certainly qualifies her to seek relief. You (men) wouldn't wait as long as women tend to before embarking on a nationwide pussy hunt to satisfy your itch. Our patience is much shorter, but instead of working out the problem, we go looking for more problems by seeking the company of the wrong woman to solve the underlying problem.

Therefore, always keep in mind, for every woman you fuck that is in a relationship, another fellow man (or woman; we cannot rule out lesbians, of course) gets fucked (this time not in a sexual sense), and be sure that what goes around comes around. Next time you could be the poor bastard that tries to understand what went wrong and why your woman has a hard time confronting you with the hurtful fact that a different dick did, or is doing, a much better job than yours.

CHOOSE YOUR PUSSY WISELY

Have you asked yourself why it is that we have such a high divorce rate nowadays? It seems most couples get together only for a limited time before pulling out the divorce card and embarking on a dirty trip to the courthouse that leaves many once-happy couples and families in smoke and ashes. Apart from the far-reaching financial implications and emotional damage that result from a divorce bout, we should keep in mind that couples with kids have an even bigger burden to bear. It's their sole responsibility if their kids suffer from severe emotional hurt, which is likely to leave an imprint on their future social behavior and mental health. We can certainly claim that we are supporting an army of lawyers and psychiatrists and ensuring their livelihood, but does it have to be that way?

I say no. Here's a metaphor: Would you consider building a house on a weak foundation? And if you did, do you actually believe it would provide the means to support a tall and imposing building? To all those who answer "NO," I say "Exactly!"

Then tell me: why is it that so many couples hook up even though they are sexually incompatible? Here's where I dive into my personal philosophy and ask you to face a harsh reality: A relationship without good sex is doomed, sooner or later, and there's nothing you can do about it. Nothing can compensate for a good fuck, and no matter how much you actually think or say you love your partner, without a mutually satisfying dick-pussy connection, your relationship is going to crumble like a building suffering from structural damage.

To all you men and women that don't agree with me – I say crap. You are just frightened or ashamed to accept the truth. One of my mentors once told me: "You know, you are a very intelligent person, but I am smart. Do you know what the difference is?" I didn't have an answer, so he explained: An intelligent person will get into trouble; because of his intelligence he will somehow manage to find a way out of the situation. A smart person just stays out of trouble.

Fucking without hot and raw sex between you and the woman you are courting just sets you up for a big disappointment. You cannot decide to use your intelligence to make it work – remember, we are responding to our deepest urges and our dick will always win the battle in the long run.

Be smart, I say. It doesn't take many fuck sessions to understand that your dick and the pussy you're pounding are not getting along. Okay, okay...so the naysayers will argue that it takes time to get to know each other and open up emotionally to improve sexual communication, etc. Crap again...it takes us humans a mere few seconds to recognize if we are attracted to another person. So how long do you need to recognize that your cock is not living up to its potential with the woman you are with? The sad thing is that we often tend to ignore our gut feeling about the worrisome situation and try to brainwash ourselves into thinking that everything is just fine.

On top of that, we convince ourselves that all the other positive female attributes outweigh the lack of hot, raw and steamy sex. EEEEHHHHHHHHH (this is the best I could come up with to imitate a strong buzzer sound) – wrong answer. Don't kid yourself. If you can't satisfy your dick at home, you'll go and search for your fix someplace else, where it is more appreciated. And still... many of us men choose to ignore our deepest intuitions and decide to remain with a woman that we know is not going to give us the hard-on we so desire. We fight a losing battle if we ignore our sexual urges and allow peer or society pressure to impose on us other values than the ones that are most important to us dick-equipped creatures. (Not that the other values aren't important; they are, but not at the expense of our primal urges.)

Is this the reason why in the animal world the male is rarely bonded to a single female – despite what Disney and Pixar try to sell us on the big screen?

In the end, what I am trying to say is that if you have tried everything to bring your sex life to a satisfying level, but have failed, it is wiser to move on and not live in a state of constant sexual frustration and imbalance. It will eat away at whatever weak foundation you have built with your woman, until one day, a mere 2 on the Richter scale will bring down everything you have built over the years. A strong relationship should be able to withstand at least an 8-level earthquake, and I believe that the formula for the concrete that can withstand a forceful quake is nothing else but a fucking good relationship with your woman. A sexually active and mutually satisfying relationship will weather the tough times during the course of a relationship.

SO...WHY AM I WRITING THIS BOOK?

I honestly believe that most men don't do what is necessary to make their sexual relationship work. This may stem from a lack of knowledge on the subject of how to please your woman and/or from a "This is the way it is" mentality, a belief that you can't change the situation. In my opinion, men have to do everything in their ability to make their sexual relationship work.

IT IS UP TO YOU TO DO EVERYTHING YOU CAN TO BRING YOUR SEX LIFE TO A SATISFYING LEVEL.

The emphasis has to be on the word EVERYTHING and most men simply don't do everything. Oh fuck off, most of you really don't – I don't know what's worse, you men that know what to do and are just too lazy or self-centered to apply your knowledge, or the majority of men that simply don't have a clue what to do because it never occurred to them to learn a little more about the female sex and what it is they like when they are getting banged by their men. Still, the worst of our kind are the ones among us that believe they know what to do, or think they are doing it, but in fact know shit about how to deeply satisfy a (their) woman.

Guys, wake up! What you often call a good fuck is nothing more than a premature ejaculation that many women would rather forget – or at best classify as a weak performance but for sure NOT as a good fuck, never mind a great one.

Therefore, in the next chapters I am going to provide some basic insights and after that dive into some more advanced techniques to help those among you that are oblivious to the ABC of how to fuck your woman into heaven.

IS FUCKING A SKILL YOU CAN LEARN?

It sure is. Of course there will always be some of us that are better at it than others – that's true for everything we do. Not everyone will become a concert pianist and not everyone will turn out to be a super stud. If you remember, I said that fucking is a true art and some of us possess a certain amount of natural talent while others have to compensate with hard work and practice. However, every man can improve his fucking skills and the idea is to reach a level that is satisfying to the woman at your side.

Again…it's of utmost importance to understand that it's not enough to satisfy your own sex drive; the same level of importance should be placed on satisfying the sexual desires of the woman in your life. Only if both parties are sexually satisfied will the path for a fruitful and long-lasting relationship be laid out. It has to be a WIN-WIN situation.

For many men it is easier to understand the principles of a successful business partnership than the underlying forces in a day-to-day partnership with the woman at their side – well then, here is some good news if you haven't fig-ured it out yet. The very same rules, principles and dynamics apply in a relationship; only a win-win situation will ensure a mutual commitment that leads to an ongoing and long-term successful partnership. If at some point one of the parties feels exploited or betrayed, the entire business venture will go down the drain. So welcome to your relationship – probably your most important business venture.

In light of this, I advise you to carefully evaluate the business proposition you call your relationship, and if you come to the conclusion that one of the parties is on the losing end, then it is time to change the equation. Otherwise you could find out that one day, to your utter surprise, your woman may decide to change her supplier and go for the dick services that promise a better return on investment.

The truth is that most men are too shy or proud to go to fuck school. It is just inconceivable to them to allow the essence of their manhood to be in question or to admit there might still be a lot they can learn about using their tool more effectively.

Most men dive into various forms of self-learning methods in the hope of finding the Holy Grail – how to fuck a woman and how to "do it right." It all starts with porn, of course. Younger men start out using porn as a quick fix to jack off and satisfy their hourly urge, but at some point all the hours of watching fucking, banging and licking turn into self-educational videos that can widen their sexual horizons, if consumed and applied in an appropriate fashion (more on this in a subsequent chapter).

Then there are the bragging stories of friends and colleagues who are more than eager to share their fuck stories with their fellow men, exaggerated, of course, and yet every listener secretly wonders if he can literally measure up to these self-proclaimed super studs. Anything is valid, in the interest of confirming alpha male status, but the educational value of these hyped-up stories is usually very low, if not completely misleading.

Hookers…how many men have lost their virginity to a professional cock-sucker? Of course it's easier to use a hooker when you want to test new waters; then if you prematurely ejaculate, like most beginners do, your shameful dysfunction (it's really just a lack of training) remains a secret and your name isn't tarnished. I cannot argue against this form of action; for some men (both young and older) it's probably the easiest or only way to experience the actual feeling of their dick penetrating a wet pussy (though with hookers I'm not too sure if the pussy is wet at all) – so at least the first and often most difficult barrier is overcome.

Of course some of us are lucky and receive help from a well-seasoned woman, who sees it as her duty to guide us on our early fuck sessions. This dream woman will show you the ropes and share with you a trick or two to get a woman's clit to swell up to the size of a cherry. Isn't this every teenager's wet dream? Hollywood, of course, has plastered movies with this type of scene – which leads us to believe that these women actually exist. They do, but don't get your hopes too high; you probably have an equal chance of winning a lottery. Of all the friends you have met in life, how many actually had an older woman massage their cock when they were younger, and how many had the pleasure of sticking their cock up the same woman's ass? ...Exactly.

Then there are books and educational videos (this time I'm not referring to porn). Although some of them offer a good read or helpful advice, many, if not most of them, are too technical (medical, psychological, etc.) and not written or produced in a way that is interesting or practical.

What I am trying to say is that there are a myriad of ways to broaden a man's (your) sexual repertoire. The sad truth, however, is that men too often laugh at what they see or hear. This stems from their insecurity, and the result is they don't process what they have been exposed to and they don't learn from it. Others simply are not comfortable with wandering into unchartered waters and they stick with their current knowledge, believing, unfortunately, that it is enough to get the job done. The harsh truth is that women – most of them, in fact – fiercely disagree; **it doesn't get the job done at all!**

Women are complex creatures and there are many ways to sexually please them. Even to those men who know a lot, I say: You don't know it all, but if you keep an open mind, you will be amazed at the wealth of information and techniques you can attain to improve your sex skills. Every day you can learn something new that might please your woman even more.

What most men don't know is that women mature sexually over the years, causing their sexuality to evolve and transform. What once might have been unpleasant, or unthinkable to ask for, may today be more than welcomed by your woman.

So my advice to you, my fellow men, is to go out and devour as much as you can on this subject. Study, practice and understand how to fuck your woman right – much of your happiness in life depends on it.

IS YOUR DICK TUNED IN TO THE RIGHT CHANNEL?

The first thing men need to do is to learn the language of women. By this, of course, I'm not referring to the verbal language, but rather to the unspoken communication that is more important than actual words. Once you master how to read the female signs, you are on your way to vastly improving your sex life and of course your woman's as well.

The biggest problem is miscommunication or no communication at all. Many men and women don't communicate effectively (or at all), and much of the problems that could be solved through honest and straightforward communication evolve into bigger problems, until at some point they become insurmountable obstacles that lead to separation.

Many couples try to salvage their broken relationship by going to couple counseling. However, when a certain threshold has been reached it is often impossible to turn back the clock. Too many things have been said and too many actions have been taken, and hurt feelings prevent the couple from tackling the root cause of the problem. So what is the root cause of a deteriorating man-woman bond? Simply put...you are not fucking enough or you are not doing it right. Basically I am telling you that you are not communicating – yup, fucking is communicating.

It's the purest form of communication, raw and honest, and you and your woman are not talking in bed or have forgotten how to talk, and by this I don't mean pillow talk. You might be speaking a different language that your woman doesn't understand, or you two might be communicating in different dialects, which will cause further miscommunication and misunderstanding. Whatever you think you know or whatever someone is telling you – the root cause for most failed relationships is sexual miscommunication.

It is imperative for men to understand and accept that women use a different language to express their needs, frustration and happiness. It is also important to recognize that both men and women are not completely honest in their conversation – we are often too ashamed of our true thoughts and emotions, and most of us want to hide our weaknesses so as not to appear inferior. On other occasions we keep our mouth shut to prevent hurting the person we love. In the long run, this dishonesty will haunt us and eventually be the main reason for sinking our relationship.

I am not telling you to go out on your first date and peel off all the protective layers you have set up to shield yourself from potential disappointments and hurtful experiences, but come on…at some point, when you have decided that this woman is worth the extra effort, and that you can see yourself fucking her for many years down the road, then it is time to get rid of your excessive armor and reveal the true man that is hiding beneath.

Before you start a conversation with your woman about your emotions, feelings and anxieties, I suggest that you first express them when you are fucking her. When we fuck we are already dismissing our first layer of protective gear – our clothes – we are naked, just as nature created us, and we are exposing many of our hidden flaws.

Of course this means you have to start fucking with the lights on!!! – don't be shy and start to accept for once who you are in real life (reality shows are very popular nowadays). It doesn't have to be broad daylight in the beginning – ambient lighting will do for starters, but it's essential to begin to express your self-confidence and also see your woman in all her glory. As much as you want her to accept you for who you are, you also need to accept her for who she is. Lowering your guard and letting her see the naked truth about you is the first step towards honest communication. Look at me…this is who I am and I see you and I appreciate everything about you. For many couples, the road already ends here – sad but true. If your relationship is ever going to be long-lasting and mutually fulfilling, both parties have to be open with each other from the get go.

Again…there will be many of you who disagree and say that "fucking" (some of you actually still have a problem using dirty words and the faster you get over it the better for you) isn't everything in a relationship.

Wrong again…it's EVERYTHING – in the sense that it's the most important thing. If you are honest when you're fucking, there is a good chance that you are also honest in your verbal conversation. To some it might appear that honesty in bed is more difficult to achieve than talking. It should be the other way around and this is what you have to work on.

Most of the time when we talk we are dressed, and women have additional protective layers – like makeup, a bra and other supporting accessories that help them to conceal their weaknesses. Without them, most of us, and especially women, are figuratively speaking naked – and yes, more vulnerable, but also definitely more honest.

Furthermore, in a conversation our head takes charge – at least most of the time, We have been taught to think before we speak, and therefore, much of what we say is the result of a conscious decision and as such it isn't raw in its nature. Raw is honest; it's the purest form of expressing ourselves verbally, but we never or rarely revert to this expressive form. In fact, many people are very articulate and speak believable words that don't represent their actual thoughts or the truth about how they feel. And sometimes we use dishonesty to talk ourselves into our woman's pants or out of an awkward situation.

However, don't be mistaken: dishonesty will leave a crack in a delicately balanced relationship that can easily turn into a breach of trust that becomes impossible to fix.

Most insecurities and anxieties start with a "What if..." and we too often tend to let these "What if's" rule our life. Here are a few scenarios (undoubtedly some of you have been there): What if she thinks my dick is too small? What if I come too fast? What if I can't make her come? And let's make it clear – women go through the same anxieties: What if he thinks my ass is too big? What if he doesn't like my tits? What if he doesn't call me after I let him fuck me? You need to understand that most "What ifs" are unsubstantiated and dissolve the instant you confront them. Confronting them will help to increase your overall state of happiness.

So back to my original advice: take a leap of faith and switch on the lights before you fuck your woman next time. It's up to us men to lead the way and help our woman understand that there's nothing we cannot handle and that we desire them no matter what. If you cannot do that, then be prepared to accept the consequences or ask yourself if you actually truly desire the woman you're with. Maybe you're just afraid that she will dislike what she sees once the lights come on – if so, how can you live with your insecurity on a daily basis? Maybe you are not aware that nature has created women in such a way that they are less influenced than men are by superficial attributes; they are more attracted to the manly values of strength, wisdom, wit, a sense of security, and here it comes – good fucking.

If you can fuck your woman in such a way that it leaves her breathless and gasping for air because she has just experienced a multiple orgasm, then a lot of common relationship maladies wouldn't stand a chance of weakening your male-female bond. A good fuck is like a strong dose of vitamin C that prevents you from catching a cold. It will strengthen the immune system of your relationship (sex also strengthens your immune system) and create a protective shield against most of the day-to-day nuisances between men and women (and there are many).

So as long as you are taking your vitamins (fucking), your relationship will be in pretty good shape. Just think about it for a moment and you'll know that I'm right. Think back to a time when your woman was annoyed at you and every little thing you did upset her. Then think back to how long it had been since you last had a great fuck – et voilà.

Okay – so now we know that we have to routinely fuck our woman in order to maintain a healthy and happy relationship – BUT it's not enough to fuck your woman every day (don't kid yourself, this rarely happens); the quality of your sexercise is critical. Most men struggle to place their performance in bed on a scale from 1 to 10, with 10 representing the ultimate fuck – and this is a big problem. We cannot ask a woman straightforward: "Tell me, how good was it on a scale of 1 to 10?" We are just too afraid to be slapped in the face with the hard truth that our self-assessment is way off the mark.

Then of course there are men who are oblivious to the fact that they completely suck in bed. These are the self-absorbed males that measure the quality of sex by male parameters: Oh yeah, I came – man, I fucked her for more than an hour – shit, I'm all sweaty – 1 really look good when I fuck her (the ones that are really full of themselves and need a mirror to get off). But sarcasm aside, many men really don't take the time to listen to their women when they fuck them.

Remember, I said that fucking is communicating? This means that both parties have to converse with each other. We men have to start to read the signs and listen to our women when we fuck them. It's the only way we will truly know if we are satisfying them or not. If you want to know what to listen for and how to read the signs, read on.

LISTEN TO THE PUSSY!

Well by now you know what I mean. We men have to carefully listen to the pussy of our woman, but it's not only the pussy that sends us unmistakable signs that we are successfully pleasing our woman. There are many signals you have to learn to pick up if you want to understand when your woman appreciates what you are doing. Sometimes it's a combination of signals that confirms that you are on the right track. Being able to pick them up early on in the game will provide you with the advantage of being able to adjust your moves if needed.

It starts way before you stick your dick into the pussy – way, way before! It is crucial that you understand this. Forcing your woman to fuck you when she isn't in the mood is just bad for your relationship; it's not a win-win situation. The only one who is going to benefit from this one-sided fuck is your dick; as for you, you will have to take into account that you have just lost additional points with your woman. Adding too many of these negative points is damaging to the overall health of your relationship and we men have to ensure that we rack up as many good points (deeds) as possible. As much as possible, you should keep the balance in favor of the good points, and hopefully after you read this book, the good ones will outweigh the bad ones by a large margin.

When I tell you it starts way, way before, I actually mean before you even have thought about taking out your dick. Women are very complex creatures and we men have to apply finesse in order to get some pussy. Getting your woman to spread her legs, give you head, ride your dick or a combination of all of the above is nothing more than a bonus – a daily, weekly or monthly bonus for outstanding performance (I really hope you fuck more than once a month; otherwise you might have a real emergency on your hands.)

Women constantly measure our performance in terms of daily accomplished deeds – this time I am not referring to the act of fucking. They do it unconsciously, at least most women do, and in response to our selflessly accomplished tasks around the house, they will switch on their fuck receptors. Just like anything else in life, you will have to work hard to get your fuck. We men are used to it – or have you already forgotten how hard y ou were working to get into her pants the first time you met her? The fact that you are in a steady relationship with this woman doesn't give you the inherent right to stick your dick in her pussy whenever you have a stiff one – and that's the hard truth. We men have to continuously work to win over our women and keep them attracted to us.

A woman will ask herself: "What has my man done to deserve my pussy?" If she cannot come up with a satisfactory answer, Pussyland stays shut. On the other hand, if you take out the trash, do the laundry, bathe the kids, and do the shopping (all in one day), a chemical reaction takes place in your woman's head and she switches on her fuck receptors. If this switch hasn't been activated, don't even bother – your woman will not get into the banging mood and it's wiser to just jerk off and forget trying to convince her to fuck you.

So the message is: make sure you work to earn your pussy time and you will be amazed at how approachable your woman suddenly becomes. Just like when you let your boss know you have done some good work, don't forget to let your woman know what you have done for her (today).

And again, be smart about it – don't just walk up to her and tell her, "I did this and I did that," because she will think, "So what? I do it every day." No, you have to be clever and subtle when pointing out your deeds. For example, when you take out the trash, don't put a new bag into the garbage pail (let her find it empty). When you do the shopping, leave a few items on the table top, and when you bathe the kids, just do it without a pre-announcement. Women like to be surprised and they want to feel that their man is providing for them – not only moneywise. They want to feel appreciated, and when you take care of day-to-day tasks, they feel that they are not alone in the relationship and that you are carrying your weight.

Most often it is the extra effort that counts; even if you mess up with some of the tasks, they still count as good deeds, just as long as you went the extra mile to contribute to the partnership. Knowing this will make your life so much easier, and it will drastically increase your opportunities to get laid.

Once you have created the basic groundwork to get fucked, you still need to push the right buttons to get your woman to accept your advances and respond to them positively. Be warned: your work isn't over yet – getting your woman from "I am in the mood" to "Fuck me now" requires more than just rubbing her pussy. You can easily kill the mood by hitting the wrong buttons or being too clumsy. Don't ruin your chance for a good fuck just because you didn't learn what your woman expects from you.

The big difference between us men and woman is that when we are stiff and ready to fuck, our women are still far behind in the race. It takes them much longer to transition the I-am-in-the-mood-for-sex feeling from the head to the pussy. Hence we must help our woman to make this journey. It is vital that you know that women fuck as much with their head as with their pussy. We men on the other hand are slaves to our dicks; especially when our best friend is all pumped up, it is he who dictates all our actions. With women, the mind still plays the central role and can abruptly crash the party. Yes, yes, our women are difficult and complex, but if we know how to handle (manipulate) them correctly, we can often get what we are after.

Let's return to signals and knowing what to look out for. Beware! Women can play you. Many of us have seen the classic movie When Harry Met Sally and have witnessed Sally's fake orgasm. We all laughed at it, but did you laugh because it was funny or because you were trying to cover up your insecurity? Did it remind you of a scene where you weren't sure if the woman you were banging was faking it?

There is no doubt that many men are fooled by fake female orgasms. I said I wouldn't quote statistics, but believe me, they're high. Some of you may have sensed that something wasn't right, but you were not able to con-firm your intuition. The general rule is that if you are sensing something fishy with your woman's reactions when you are banging her, then you are probably right. It also means that you are sensitive enough to recognize some of the warning signals (congratulations!) and you can apply appropriate counter measures.

Nevertheless, most men, even if they sense something's off track, tend to ignore these intuitive feelings and let their dick carry on. What they should do is react to the signals and adjust their course of action so they can end up with a win-win fuck scenario. Don't ignore the signals if you already possess the gift of being able to recognize them; use them to your advantage.

I assure you that if we men know how to read the signs, we will not be fooled by fake orgasms and foul play. It's about time you know how to recognize the signals that will help you figure out on your own whether your woman is having an orgasm or whether she is just pretending.

Putting the orgasm aside for a second, I even go so far as to claim that it is more important that you sense if she is enjoying the fuck itself. There are many proverbs that try to capture what I am trying to convey, such as: "It is good to have an end to the journey, but it is the journey that matters in the end" or "The journey is the reward." Whichever one you prefer, they all point to the fact that the fucking part can often be better than the orgasm itself. If I look back at many of my great fucks, I hardly remember the orgasm part, but I can remember the details of the fuck: where it took place, what positions we tried out, the expression on her face, the smell of her pussy, and so forth. The actual climax is something we tend to forget as they are often very similar.

On the other hand, women remember good orgasms more than we do, as they experience them all too rarely. We men come 99% of the time when we fuck, but we should try extra hard not to shoot our load before our woman reaches her orgasm.

If your woman doesn't reach her climax, she will most likely classify the experience as just another disappointing fuck in which she was merely a tool to satisfy your urge. However, there are exceptions to the rule; women with a high orgasm ratio are more likely to accept a fuck that didn't hit the ball out of the park. They will not stamp it right away as another disappointing fuck in a series of disappointing fucks.

Women themselves know that they are hard to satisfy sexually and that they need a longer period of time to reach an orgasm, which is why they cut us men some slack, but only to a certain point. We have to get our act together or they will gradually loose respect for us (and our dick) and from that point onwards it's a downhill slope. Don't be mistaken; the general rule still is: make sure the pussy comes and if possible more than once!

Think of a message being transmitted using the Morse code. All the dots and dashes only translate into a comprehensible message when they are connected. Of course you still need to learn how to read the Morse code to understand the message. The nice thing about the Morse code is that if you know it, you don't have to write it down to understand the message. A trained ear can easily connect the rapid succession of sounds in real time and translate them into meaningful words. The same is true when you are fucking your woman. She constantly sends out signals that you have to translate into words and you should be able to encode them on the fly – *communication, communication*; I cannot repeat it enough.

Some men have problems with multitasking – specifically they have problems performing a physical task (fucking) and a mental task (translating the code) simultaneously. If you want to step up your game and impress your woman, it means that you have to be able to lick pussy, use one hand to play with her tits and finger her pussy with the remaining free hand all at once. You will have to overcome this deficiency if you want to excel at pleasing your woman – it's worth it.

THE FUCKING CODE

So much talk about signals...so what are they? This chapter provides insight into the most common signals and aims to help you to decipher the messages your woman is sending when you are fucking her.

Body language – for the men not familiar with this very important topic, I strongly recommend you dive deeper into this subject and learn how to read the signs our bodies are continually sending out. There are many good books and internet sites on this subject, so there is no excuse not to expand your horizon on this issue. I am going to touch only on the basics. They might be obvious to some of you, but even these basic signals are often not picked up or are disregarded by the majority of men.

The reasons are usually simple ignorance or deliberate selfishness. Men in general, need to be more observant about their woman's body language and be able to correctly evaluate the situation before heading into battle to conquer the pussy. Too many battles are lost before you even set foot on the battleground, and choosing the right battle accounts for half the victory.

Look out for the following: Is your woman sitting close to you? If not, it is more difficult (although not impossible) to trigger the fuck receptors in her head. Without body contact, it is much more difficult to express your physical intent. Women very much appreciate touch before getting fucked; it eases them into the idea of having to blow you.

Let's assume your woman is sitting close to you – how would you describe her posture? Is her body or parts of it, like her legs, chest or face, turned to face your direction? Do you have any body contact? Does she place her hands, legs or head on you? If the answer is yes to any of these questions, you have a good starting point. If the answer is no, you have to approach her carefully and try to engage her. If she accepts your advances and reciprocates your actions – for example when you start caressing her back, her thighs, or the back of her neck, or start playing with her hair, and she doesn't reject you, then you are in a favorable position. Any repelling sign, such as the slightest physical withdrawal, a grimacing facial expression, or a verbal rebuke, means you have to proceed with more caution. We men have to be tenacious in our quest to satisfy our urge, but we also have to know when to give in and call it a day. If all your caressing and subtle approaches don't work – then don't bother. You're going to jerk off tonight and the earlier you accept it and return to watching TV, the faster your dick is going to let you rest.

Some of you will argue that much of what I suggest is apparent, and that you've heard it all before. Well, for most men it's still news, and even though many may pick up the signs of rejection, they still try hard to convince their woman that it is in their own best interest to fuck them now. Not clever, not clever at all in the long run. Even if you are able to talk your woman into fucking you now, it's on your own terms in order to satisfy your rebelling dick, and that's not a win-win situation.

Still…and there's a big still, I urge you to remember your dating days and think of how many times the woman you dated didn't want to fuck with you on a first or second date, but in the end you managed to get into her pants. We men are hunters, it's in our genes, and what I want to say is that we should never give up without a fight. The experienced and enduring hunter will always try to catch his prey, and he will pull out every trick in his repertoire to try and get his trophy – juicy pussy. On the other hand, it's just part of life that the hunter often returns empty handed. Not every hunting party ends with a kill and a full stomach. Don't be too hard on yourself, and don't blame your woman if she didn't take the bait. Just make sure to go out the next day and try again.

Know that your woman doesn't forget that she rejected you, and if she does it once, twice or even three times in a row, eventually she will give in to her nagging conscience and grant you a pity fuck (provided you still have a relationship of some sorts). We men need to make sure our woman never grants us pity fucks, as once again it's not a win-win scenario. She will spread her legs, but she will do it reluctantly, which automatically means that she is not going to enjoy it as much as she should. Many men are just happy to jump at the chance to stick their throbbing cock into a wet pussy and they neglect to read the underlying signs. In my younger years, that was me, eager to jump at every pussy that presented the chance of granting my dick relief. But it's a very different story once you have chosen to enter a relationship. The entire game plan changes and it becomes a matter of quality versus quantity. Of course, if you can have both, all the better – consider yourself a very lucky (or smart) chap.

Today I cannot count the times I have walked away from a pity fuck. Honestly, I really don't enjoy fucking my woman if she isn't enjoying it as well. It's like stale soup missing the salt, and hey, I like salt. To all my fellow men I recommend following this course of action: whenever you sense that your woman is offering you a pity fuck, just tell her (in a polite way, of course) no thanks. Let her know that you don't want a one-sided fuck that only you are going to enjoy. Believe me, your woman is going to respect you for that and you will definitely gain some good points. Remember that the good points convert into rewarding fucks. I would trade any two or three mediocre fucks for one great one.

As mentioned earlier, I believe we should at least try to apply persuasive techniques to see if we can turn on the fuck switch in our woman's head. The subtle approach is only one of several methods you can use to test the waters; the truth is we often don't know in advance what kind of mood our woman is in. Sometimes a more direct approach is needed to spark her pussy juices. Depending on the situation, I sometimes like to walk up to her and press her close to me so she can feel my hard on, and then grab on to her ass with both hands to push her even closer. This has to be accompanied by passionate kisses – don't forget to use the tongue after a few warm-up kisses. Some couples really forget to kiss, or they don't do it enough. Kissing is very sexual, and there's nothing like a good kiss to get your brain waves all stirred up and your cock rock hard. With women, kissing is even more important. Kissing is an exchange of intimacy, and without intimacy women simply do not enjoy sex that much (if at all). It's also the best way to find out if your advances are appreciated. If she reacts with passionate kisses and is ready to stick her tongue all the way up into your mouth, then the ground is well prepared for taking the next steps.

In addition to your physical approach, you have to use words – the right words. Here I don't refer to smootchie pootchie sweet talk. No, in this case it has to be the hard core stuff, words that unmistakably make it clear to your woman that you desire her on the deepest and rawest level and that all you have on your mind this very moment is to bend her over and fuck her hard. Remember, women like to be surprised and even the best-brought-up lady wants to step into the role of a disreputable whore once in a while. More on how to talk dirty in another chapter (yes, this also needs to be done with a touch of finesse).

Now we are getting somewhere – you and your woman have reached a mutual understanding that you both want to fuck – good for you – but now you have to continuously watch out for the signals that could warn you that you are not in breach of that agreement. If there is one lesson you should learn, it's to take your time. Don't rush to get naked and hump your woman. Although occasionally this can be just the type of fuck both of you want, the general rule is to take it slowly and build up the desire.

However, sometimes the timing is not right. Your woman may still have unfinished business on her mind, and as long as she hasn't completed her mental to-do list, it will get in the way of your sexual advances. She might want to take care of herself first. For example, she may want to take a shower and pamper herself with a cosmetic do-over (nails, hair, peeling, etc.). Maybe the kids are not asleep yet, or she is still in the middle of cooking, or she is watching her favorite TV show. If this is the case, then you have to pull back and wait for the right moment. You have already sent her a clear message that you want to fuck her and that you are counting on it at the earliest possible time. Give her the space to complete whatever she has to do, and then wait for the right moment to rekindle the passion. Your hope is to pick up where you left off earlier.

If your game plan doesn't work out, don't be frustrated. Your woman still may not be in the right mood to fuck you, even though she has had the time to tend to all her needs. The one need that she might lack is rest. Our women also need time to relax and recharge their batteries, and maybe tonight's the night – you cannot always win, and that's a fact. Sometimes you just get hit with a reality check.

But for now, let's carry on with the positive scenario: your woman is not too exhausted to have sex so what you are striving for is for your woman to reach a point where she simply wants to fuck you and is ready to do almost anything to satisfy you (and her). How do we do that?

FOREPLAY, FOREPLAY AND FOREPLAY!!

This basic concept is still a foreign language for most men and they don't seem to care enough to study it. What a shame – you fucking don't know what you're missing because it's an essential element in the communication with your woman. Foreplay is such an important topic that I am dedicating a full chapter (later) to the subject so you know what women need and what they hope to get from their men.

So now you're kissing passionately and your hands start to explore the private regions of your woman. Make sure to kiss for a while and really get into it – it's an intrinsic part of a woman's warm-up phase. Make sure your woman keeps close body contact and that she doesn't disapprove of your hard on rubbing against her crotch. Any sign of that means you might have to gear down a bit and invest more time in the kissing phase and the exploration of her body. Don't grab her ass right away. Try to hold her tight, preferably around the waist with one hand on the back of her neck to let her know that you are in control of the situation and that she can let herself go. Women want to know that their men are physically able to protect them; only then are they able to let go completely. To make your woman feel safe and protected means that you have to hold, move and place her body in ways that assure her that you are always in control of the situation (fuck).

After you make certain that your scaled-back approach is bearing fruit, then move on to her ass. First caress it, feel the roundness of her butt checks before you start grabbing them. Start softly before you tighten your grip. If she accepts this, you can proceed.

Tits! Now pay attention. Please be gentle. Stroke them without touching the skin. Do you feel her nipples hardening? Yeah? That's a good sign. She is getting there. Now you can reach under her bra and start to gently play with her nipples (read on if you want to know how to play correctly with her tits). Don't forget to kiss her – many men suddenly forget to kiss and focus all their attention on the tits and ass and that's a big mistake – you're not there yet. Reach into the back of her pants and feel her butt checks. Insert your fingers into her crack and if she isn't dismissive reach under the panties and feel her asshole. Now focus on her pussy and reach between her legs – from outside her panties. Gently rub and massage her pussy area. Are you sensing that she is breathing harder? Are her eyes closed? Is she accepting everything you do to her? Is she moving her hips in sync with your rubbing and massaging hand motion? These are the signs you have to watch out for.

Unbutton her pants – and insert your hand into her pants. No need to reach under her panties yet. Feel her pussy through the panties and play with it – gently at first and then slightly increase your finger pressure. Squeeze her pussy lips between your thumb and index finger. Are you feeling the wetness of her pussy penetrate the panties? This is a very good sign – don't stop. Are you still kissing her? Just reminding you!

At this point, most men lose patience and start to move too fast. Our dicks are rock hard and the only thing we can think of is fucking her. Why the rush? Enjoy it; the longer you wait the better the fuck will be in the end.

So now she is wet. Move your hands underneath her panties and feel the wet flesh. Is she spreading her legs? Is she giving herself to you? Now be aware. If your finger technique is clumsy, she will cramp up, which means she is not enjoying it. You might be hurting her or you might simply not be hitting the right spots. Sadly, many women accept the fact that their men do not know better, and instead of enduring awkward foreplay they would rather move on to the next phase and get it over with. Not a good sign. So you get fucked, but from this point onwards the result is already one-sided and tainted. The dick may have scored a short-term win – Yiha – but don't get too enthusiastic about it; long-term-wise you've just put another nail into your relationship's coffin.

Look at her face. Are her eyes still closed and is her face still showing the glow of horniness? No? Bad sign – your foreplay sucks and now we're back to the pity fuck. Read on and learn what you are doing wrong.

But for now, let's say your woman is still in the mood and you are actually not too clumsy at what you're doing (this still doesn't mean that you can't do better), which means you are moving on to the next level and about to get undressed. Is she undressing you? Good sign. Does it seem like she can't get out of her clothes fast enough? Is she ripping them off and throwing them all over the place? Great sign – she's horny and doesn't care about making a mess.

On the other hand, do you notice you're doing most of the work? Do you have to get her undressed? Is her face showing signs of "if it must be"? Bad signs. Be attentive to these nuances; they mean the difference between a great fuck, a mediocre fuck, and a fuck that sucks. Once her pants are off, make sure she keeps her panties on for a little longer – build up the tension – and continue working her pussy through her panties until you feel they are dripping wet from her pussy juice. Continually watch her face to see if she is enjoying what you're doing, and if you have doubts, apply slight changes (meaning stroke her pussy faster, slower, harder, softer...) until you witness an improved look on her face.

If your emotional sensors are deficient or rusty, don't be afraid to ask her if she likes what you're doing or if she prefers something else. Many couples have to start from scratch and build a basic understanding as to what constitutes a good fuck in their partner's eyes. So communicate verbally until you can read each other's body language. It's far better than groping in the dark and basically "fucking up." Being shy at this point is just plain stupid. By now you should know this woman and have seen her naked more than enough times – so there's no reason to be awkward. Overcome whatever fear you have and seize the opportunity to show her that you are strong enough to care about what she wants from your hands, tongue and dick.

Let's continue...is she pressing your hand against her pussy? Is she playing with her tits – preferably is she pinching her nipples until they're hard? Is her mouth half open and is her breathing heavier? Are her legs spread even wider? Does she start to play with her pussy or assist you in fingering her pussy? Is she licking her lips? Does she moan? Does she shiver slightly? Does she reach for your cock and if it is out in the open, does she start to stroke you? Are her kisses still as passionate?

All of the above are good signs and they mean that her sexual tension is building. The longer you can extend this foreplay the better. These signs can come in any combination and several need to occur to confirm that you are on the right track. A woman can easily fake some of these signals, but not all of them simultaneously. Be prepared to accept if something is not working out, but rather than seeing it as a catastrophe, open up a dialogue and find out what you can both do to improve the situation. Your woman will be appreciative if she feels that you are genuinely concerned and that you are thinking of her rather than your dick.

Let's move on – many of these signs are repetitive at various stages of what I like to call the fuck cycle. When you eat her pussy (I certainly hope you do, as this is a must to bring a woman to new heights and I dedicate a lot of pages to instruct you on how to do it right), does she push your face deep into her pussy? Does she grab on to your hair? Does she open her pussy so you can better lick her? Does she play with her pussy while you lick her? Is she still playing with her tits? Is her moaning getting louder? Is she moving her hips up and down? When you look at her face (without stopping your tongue action of course), do you see the lust on her face? Does she want to return the favor and suck your dick? Lick your balls? Stick a finger up your ass?

So far, so good. When it comes to finally fucking your woman – is she telling you to stick your dick into her pussy?

Does she talk dirty? Does she bite or scratch when you thrust your cock into her? Does she grab onto your ass and push you hard into her? Does she stick a finger in her ass when you fuck her? Is she screaming or moaning loud? All of these are good signs of course.

Now you still need to be cautious – when you fuck her, is her pussy still wet? Many women can pretend that they like your dick action, but the pussy can't lie. If you sense it's drying out, it means either that she already peaked (women can peak without coming, which we have to avoid) or that she just wants it to be over.

Peaking can occur when your woman is close to reaching her orgasm but she doesn't reach it, as you are not able to push her over the edge. It's like seeing the finish line on the final stretch of a 1,500 meter run and realizing that you haven't divided your strength appropriately and you're unable to complete the final dash to win the race. We men need to understand that one of the more frustrating things for a woman is being close to an orgasm and not being able to reach it. If this happens too often, it's very frustrating for her, and your woman could lose confidence in your ability to sexually satisfy her – meaning "Baby, you don't know how to fuck me right."

Look out for other signs of disappointment: Are her nipples flat? Is her face showing signs of "When is this over?" Has she stopped being active, meaning is she moving her thighs less than before? Or worse, is she just lying there? When you are taking her from behind, is she just giving her ass to you without responding to your pounding cock? When she is on top you, is she just sitting and waiting for you to bang her or is she riding your cock?

Is she suddenly quieter? Any one of these signals means she has peaked or she is not enjoying the ride. You then have four options to choose from:

One - you don't give a damn and continue until you shoot off your load, in which case you add negative points and worsen your overall fuck rating.

Two - you stop the awkward situation and retire from this fuck session with dignity. Your woman will be surprised at your selfless act and it will add to your good points.

Three - you can decide to stop fucking her and ask her if you can jerk off on her ass, pussy or tits – whichever you prefer. This is a good compromise and if you haven't jerked off on your woman yet, you will be surprised to know that it can arouse her to see you yank vehemently at your cock while you ask her to spread her pussy or open her butt cheeks for a better view of her fuck holes.

Four - try to rekindle the sex drive in your woman by doing things she doesn't expect of you or turning back the fuck action to a more gentle and foreplay-type session so she can refocus her mind and get back in stride. Women can experience multiple orgasms, so there is no reason why they can't get back in the saddle if they are taken care of in the right way. Often she will appreciate the extra effort you have put in to turn a disappointing fuck into a climaxing act, and if you succeed you're the man – her man – and she will respect you more. And that's where you want to be in your relationship.

Okay. We still haven't looked at the signals for spotting a genuine orgasm as opposed to a fake one. Some signs are so obvious and still men struggle to recognize them. Even worse, they don't stop to question the validity of the entire fuck session, even if no positive signals occur. Maybe some men honestly believe their women cannot experience orgasm, as no matter what they try, she just doesn't come. I am not questioning your true motives if you really try hard to give your woman the orgasm she deserves, but come on – have you ever asked yourself if the problem could be you? – or better said, your incompetency to fuck your woman the way she needs to be fucked?

Well, take heart. It's not too late (I always try to keep a positive attitude and look at the half-full glass) to turn things around and become a man who knows how to satisfy his woman. Many men, as I mentioned earlier, are too self-absorbed to even notice that the signals are missing, and this is discouraging.

Here are some of the signals women send out when they experience an orgasm and any one of these is enough to confirm that your woman just came. (Of course there are certain women that are able to control their bodily functions at such a level that they can still mislead you – but luckily for us men they are in the minority; most women have better things to do than invest time in training their pussy muscles to send us misleading signals.)

So what's a home run? Without any doubt, a squirting pussy. Yeah, female ejaculation – this is something every man and woman should strive to achieve. A squirting woman is a woman that experiences the best orgasms, and for us men there cannot be any doubt that we hit the right spots. So embrace it when your woman squirts all over the bed sheets, carpet or sofa. It is a testimony that you are fucking her right and she is really enjoying it!

Still, this doesn't mean that you have no room for improvement (most men are still weak performers in certain pre- or post-fuck areas), but it's definitely the signal you are hoping to get when you are fucking your woman. Your woman doesn't always need to shoot a fountain of pussy juice into the air to let you know she just experienced a fantastic orgasm. Many times she will only be extremely wet and occasionally she will drip, which can be very similar to squirting (learn more on how to make your woman squirt in the following chapter). Often, when you are fucking your woman doggy style and her pussy is very wet, then it can easily happen that you pump air into her pussy with every thrust, and this might result in a pussy fart. Don't be offended or irritated by these sounds. Accept them as good signs and please let your woman know that she has no reason to be embarrassed at her farting pussy. I, for example, get turned on by these sounds. I encourage my woman to relax her pussy even more so she can fully enjoy the fuck and let out as many of these farting sounds as possible.

What else? Any more signals to watch out for? Yup – pussy spasms. Definitely a good sign – they occur when your woman comes, whether it is your dick or your tongue that gives her the pleasure. Be proud of your achievement and clap yourself on the back, as she has just experienced an orgasm. If you do it right, it can turn into a multiple orgasm. Another good sign is when her asshole contracts or expands. Again my fellow men, these are good signs. Welcome them, as they undisputedly tell you that your woman is enjoying herself and has reached an orgasm.

Without a doubt, any of the above-mentioned signs guarantee that your woman is digging your dick action and no matter what you believe or what she says – these signs cannot be faked. Moaning, screaming, scratching and verbal announcements about an upcoming orgasm can all be easily faked. However, in combination with one of the non-fake signals they are an indication of your woman's pleasure level. Whenever you fuck your woman, make sure to watch out for these signals, and if you don't see them, be inspired to make them happen.

One last thing to mention: women don't always need to experience an orgasm to enjoy the fuck – unlike us men. Some women are handicapped by a mental block that denies them the relaxation needed to experience an orgasm; this can stem from anxieties or negative experiences.

Over time we may be able to make our woman feel comfortable enough so she can experience the intimacy she needs to relax and lose control. In the meantime, she may still enjoy the fuck session even though she doesn't have an orgasm. Make sure you talk to her about what she needs and be sensitive to the signals she sends you. Depending on how well you know your woman or on how open your relationship is, she might have shared with you the reasons that cause the block. Sometimes a good portion of honesty might be just the remedy needed to fix this as it might help to resolve problems that have piled up over the years and hindered her from enjoying herself. However, if the reasons are on a deeper psychological level, you might want to consider convincing your woman to seek professional help to overcome her barriers. In this case, make sure you are considerate and compassionate in your efforts.

FOUNTAIN OF JOY

Female ejaculation. I promised to elaborate more on this subject, as I genuinely believe that most couples out there (i.e., men and women alike) are not adequately educated on the subject of female ejaculation and are ignorant about the fact that every woman can ejaculate if she really enjoys being fucked. Added to this are the completely wrong conclusions that are formed when a woman squirts during sex.

My humble opinion on this issue is that it is every man's obligation to educate himself on this subject and attain the proper technique to ensure that his woman can experience the ultimate sexual pleasure. Think of it like drilling for oil, with the difference that you know where to dig to hit the well. Every time your woman squirts, you will know that you made her come in the best possible way and that she sees you as the master of her pussy. Squirting women are very happy women; they enjoy sex, are sexually satisfied, and are overall more content, which is important for a good, healthy relationship.

Occasionally men hit the well of sexual happiness by chance, meaning they don't know what they did that made their woman squirt all over the place. This lack of knowledge (of the female anatomy) can turn into a negative experience and cause shame and insecurity in your woman if your reaction is shock and disgust when you are confronted with the sudden and uncontrollable release of bodily fluids from your woman's pussy. To all the men that have reacted repulsively to this natural sexual phenomenon, I say: you idiots. The shame should be all yours. Do yourself a big favor and crawl back to your woman and apologize for your stupidity and ignorance.

So how do you make your woman squirt? First of all, it helps to know what causes it. In short, it's the stimulation of the G-spot that makes her express her joy by releasing tons of bodily fluid. Uhhh, you may think – G-spot, I've heard of it.

Good, and now you will learn how to find and stimulate it. The G-spot is an area 1 to 1.5 inches across and is located in the upper region of the vagina. It's just a little behind the entrance to your woman's pussy at the back of the pubic bone. Women will have trouble finding it on their own, because it's quite tricky to reach due to the unfavorable angle. (Maybe now you understand why some sex toys come in a U-shape and why they are described as G-spot stimulators.) However, we men can easily reach this spot and there are certain finger techniques you should learn in order to find and stimulate the G-spot and make your woman squirt like a fountain.

You need to reach deep and use the entire length of your fingers (unless you have exceptionally long fingers) to find the spot. You can easily identify the G-spot, because it actually feels like a little sponge (notice the different texture of the G-spot compared to the surrounding tissue), and when you start to stimulate this area, the tissue (sponge) fills up with fluid.

A woman that has never squirted before might mistake squirting for urinating, as it originates almost in the same area. This may cause a woman to feel ashamed without reason and men to question if their woman just peed on them. Well, now at least you know that it's not urine. You just need to smell it to know it's different. Urine has a pungent smell as we all know, whereas squirt juice has a kind of sweet aroma. Furthermore, physically speaking, women cannot squirt and pee at the same time, as their urinating canal (urethra) temporarily closes up – so relax!

Amazingly, no one knows to date what these fluids are, where they exactly originate, or what their actual purpose is, but with certainty it can be said that they are neither urine nor vaginal fluids and that they have no lubricating effect. In my opinion the real purpose of women squirting is to give us an unmistakable sign that they just came.

Here are some additional facts you should be aware of. Did you know that a G-spot-induced orgasm with ejaculation is much like the male orgasm? It induces physical fatigue and the need for a refractory period. (I know I promised not to throw around any medical expressions, but I think this one is useful: The refractory period is the recovery phase after an orgasm, during which it is physiologically impossible for an individual to have additional orgasms.) However, many women are capable of experiencing multiple orgasms (as we know), and for sure it is possible for your woman to squirt and squirt and squirt – the question is whether the massive amount of ejected fluid is a result of a single or multiple orgasm. I like to call this a problem of the rich, as it really doesn't matter – what matters is that your woman experienced a fantastic orgasm or many.

Every woman is different, of course, and the number of squirts and the amount of ejected fluid are individually determined. So does every woman have a G-spot and is every woman able to squirt? There is no real answer to this question, and even scientists have different opinions, but you should do your own experiment to find out the truth about your woman. You will have to practice and not get discouraged if you don't hit the right spot the first time around.

Know that some women only develop the ability to squirt as they mature with age. I believe that has to do with the fact that they are more comfortable with their body and that they are more relaxed when they are being fucked, which effectively lets them enjoy sex more.

What do you need to know to stimulate the G-spot to make it squirt? The answer is: patience and tender play followed by forceful vaginal handling (some women may require vaginal fisting to spurt, but I will share with you some other techniques that may work just as well). Start stimulating the G-spot by tenderly massaging it with your index and middle fingers. Push your fingers deep into your woman's pussy and search for the tissue that feels a little different. You should feel the soft tissue fill up (swell) as you massage it more and more. Use your thumb to play with the clit while your fingers inside her pussy continue to stimulate the G-spot. For many women, stimulating the G-spot is more exciting than the external clit massage, but having you tend to both simultaneously gets your woman intensely horny. You will notice that the more you massage the G-spot, the wider the pussy expands. Now you should be able to gradually insert more fingers. Make sure to do this gently, so as not to hurt your woman.

For most women, three fingers is more than enough, but find out just how many fingers she is willing to take on – it may be three or four or the entire hand. The vaginal tissue is very sensitive and a good tip is to make sure your fingernails are trimmed. Depending on how wet your womanalready is, you might be able to skip the lubricant to get deep into your woman's pussy, but just in case, have it ready next to you, so you can apply it if needed. Anothertip is to ensure that the lubricant is warmed up beforeuse, as it can be uncomfortable for the woman if the cold fluid comes in contact with the extremely stimulated and tender vaginal area.

Once you are inside your woman you have to continuously stimulate the area until you feel her vaginal muscles contracting around your fingers, hand or wrist, which is the first sign of an upcoming orgasm (this might require you to pump up the volume, which means you will find yourself vehemently hand fucking your woman at a very high tempo). A contracting pussy is the sign you are waiting for and is your signal to change position. As already mentioned, leave at least two fingers in the vagina and place your thumb over the clit and squeeze it gently. Now simply squeeze the G-spot from behind to squeeze out the liquid.

Some women don't require squeezing out the liquid and might squirt on their own. A great technique is to have your woman turn onto her stomach and lift her ass a little to open up her pussy even more. Now use your thumb to do all the pumping action. If you haven't noticed, your thumb is just the right G-spot stimulation tool. All you need is to stick it in and angle it slightly so it rubs along the back of the pubic bone and then you have to go full throttle and pump like mad. If your woman is stimulated enough, she will come in a matter of seconds and the juices will start flowing or spraying out of her vagina.

Depending on how much fluid the G-spot soaked up, it can easily result in a forceful ejaculation that can spray a few feet high (I think it's very sexy). Whatever you do now, don't stop! The orgasm will not only be very, very intense; it is possible it will turn into a multiple orgasm. Your woman will squirt again and again and she will ask you to stop, but don't. This orgasm can easily last for several minutes and there is much more fluid to come. Some women will enjoy it so much that they will demand you continue with your hand routine to make them squirt over and over again.

Don't be alarmed, but your woman's movements can be extremely forceful, uncontrolled and even spasmodic. One thing's for sure: this will be the type of orgasm she has never experienced before. You should also be aware that the orgasmic contractions can reach a level similar to those that women experience when giving birth. This can result in a painful experience if your fist is stuck up your woman's pussy when she's coming. If she is experiencing pain, simply remove a finger or two to reduce the tension, but try to keep the rest of your fingers inside her so as to retain the full effect of the stimulation.

As a last tip, based on what I already mentioned in an earlier chapter, you might want to have several towels on hand that you can spread out under your woman. Your sheets, sofa or carpet may well get soaked with squirt fluid (You might not believe this until you actually experience it firsthand).

I once again ask you to be sensitive about the fact that some women may feel ashamed or vulnerable after they experience their first squirting orgasm. They will probably react in ways that you have never witnessed before. Some women will shout or burst out in animal-like roars when they come, and they might wonder what you might think of all that. Your main job now is to immediately comfort her, hold her and tell her that you loved every minute of it and that you are happy she was able to experience such an intense orgasm. Make her feel secure and let her know that everything between you two is good and even better.

Keep in mind that many women are unaware of the vaginal orgasm. They are often only familiar with the clitoral-induced (external) orgasm, and an internal (G-spot-triggered) orgasm is quite different. However, one thing's for sure: once your woman has experienced a vaginal orgasm, nothing – I repeat nothing – will feel as intense or satisfying to her.

KING OF THE CASTLE

Not to be confused with wake me up in the morning... but then again, why not? To all of my fellow men who think only of work when the alarm clock goes off – please, take a few minutes to enjoy your morning stiffness.

Use it to surprise your woman and if she is still asleep, try to wake her gently and let her feel your hard-on. If she sleeps on her side, then spoon her and let her feel your hard cock between her legs. You will be surprised at how many times this can result in a morning fuck – morning sex is good – there's nothing more refreshing and it's a fantastic way to start a new day. So why are lots of men not doing it? Maybe you are already at work in your head, or you may think: what about the kids? (Don't let the kids get in the way of your sex life and for sure don't use them as an excuse for why your sex life sucks.) Or you may be too afraid to wake up your woman: What will she think of me? Is she going to be in the mood for it? Most likely she will rebuff me. So fucking what! No pain, no gain. Always keep trying. It never hindered you when you were single. Have you already forgotten how many times you were rejected when you made a pass at a woman?

The odds only improve slightly when you're in a relationship, even if you are with the same woman for a long time. Sure you don't have to go hunting for female ass anymore – but even with the pussy living under the same roof you will still end up with a negative record. For every fuck you get, you will receive many more rejections. That's life and the sooner you understand this, the better for you. So try to fuck your woman whenever and wherever you can.

True to the proverb, every dog has his day; we never know when we might find our woman in that sweet spot that guarantees us a good lay – all we can do is try and hope for the best. I would also like to point out that you can steer your luck a little by breaking the routine gig through a change of location. Fucking isn't limited to your bed only, you know. Hell no!

The bed is a good place, but don't get me wrong, it's a comfort zone. You need to leave it once in a while to experience something extraordinary – only then can you really appreciate the intimacy of the four corners of your bed. There are so many great places at home where you can fuck your woman and you should make it your goal to fuck her at least once in every room in your home. The only exception I can accept is to refrain from taking it to your kid's room. We still like to think of this place as an oasis of innocence. But don't be mistaken; it depends on how old your kids are and for all you know they could be experiencing more fun sex than you do.

Nonetheless, it's a statement – we own this house and we will do it wherever we want. Sex is not confined to our bed and we will let our lust run free. For many men (or couples), leaving the bed to fuck is equal to taking a big step outside, but as the Chinese say, one step at a time is good walking. So for starters you can lean your woman over the edge of the bed and take her from behind or place her on the edge of the bed and fuck her while standing (you'll be amazed how much more powerfully you perform standing up). This way you're still in the comfort zone of your bed, but you have extended the boundaries just a little. Maybe you'll take her on the floor lying next to the bed or have her kneel on a chair that is in your bedroom and enjoy the sight of her round ass. You can also sit her on the dresser and fuck her. There are so many options you can explore in this one room that will bring a change to your sex life.

The next step is to take it out of the bedroom and branch out to the remaining rooms in your home. Let's start with the bathroom. Have you ever fucked your woman while she was putting on her make up? You can approach her from behind and start to arouse her by caressing her ass and gently playing with her tits. This works whether she is dressed or naked. If she is dressed, there is nothing more arousing then pulling down her pants and panties and fucking her from behind, while you are both looking in the mirror. Just look at her face and see how beautiful she is and how her face is glowing when she is receiving some love action she didn't expect.

What about shower sex? Many men fantasize about it and don't realize it. Why? Just jump into the shower with your woman and act as nonchalantly as possible, as if it is the most natural thing to do. Now...don't get down to it right away, build up the sexual tension. There is nothing more exciting then feeling the warm water trickle down on you and feeling the naked skin of your woman in a confined space. Kiss her gently and start to soap her body. Don't be shy; get on your knees to soap her from toe to head – she'll love it. You can even offer to wash her hair. When you soap her body, make sure to give extra attention to her private parts – pussy and ass of course, and don't forget to soap her tits as well.

Now kiss! And if you get an erection make her notice! If she doesn't respond immediately (some women are shy and maybe your woman is just too overwhelmed by your newfound courage), ask her to soap your dick. Once she does, you have two options: either you enjoy a sensual hand job or you turn her around and take her from behind – it's safer this way as you wouldn't want to slip. Another safe way is to lie down in the tub on the floor of the shower and to do it in positions that are possible within the limits of the confined space.

Next on my list is the living room – sadly it is often the place that spoils the sexual tension, as this space is ruled by the TV. Although I love to sit with my woman and watch my favorite TV shows, it can easily kill any aspirations towards a sexual encounter. Therefore, you will have to fight the feeling to succumb to the mind-soothing video stream of the tube and ignite your sexual tension by finding the one thought that gets your dick up and ready for action. It's not that difficult after all. Another, less subtle way is to pop in a porn flick (make sure it's tasteful as you don't want to frighten your woman) or tune into a show with lots of sexual tension (Californication jumps to mind; it works great for women) and make your intentions clear.

The living room...what a playground to explore new and fun ways to fuck your woman. The couch itself provides a multitude of positions to completely and utterly satisfy your woman. The big difference compared to the bed is that you have more control – I love to take my woman from behind when she kneels on the floor with her body resting on the couch – the ass doesn't get much rounder and I can stare for minutes at this beautiful sight. Just wonderful! Then she can kneel on the sofa and hold on to the back rest. This way you can fuck her from behind while you are standing up – this gives you extra control of your movement and increases the power of your thrusts. You should reach for her tits and squeeze them, nipples and breasts alike, and one of my favorite acts is to reach over between her legs and play with her pussy and clit while my dick is inside her. I promise you, your women will love this and it will help her to reach an orgasm more easily.

The sofa or armchair is a great place to let her ride you or give you a blowjob. Just sit down and let her kneel in front of you to suck your cock or ask her to sit on your dick, while you grab on to her butt. You can assist her by placing your hands under her butt cheeks and help her to ride your cock. You can also place your hands on her waist, and each time she moves down, push her onto your cock to intensify the thrust. She should appreciate it. On the other hand, don't be too lazy. You should alternate between getting fucked and returning the favor. You can hold her butt and slightly elevate it to give you some room – I even like to spread her cheeks wide open – and then you push your dick upwards to fuck her deep and hard.

Start with deep and slow strokes before you up the tempo and become a piston in the engine of a muscle car. It's now up to your hips and abs to do most of the work. Move both of your hands to her pussy and spread it slightly, feeling your dick slide in and out. Also play with her asshole; massage it gently without sticking your finger in, and only when you think she is relaxed enough, gently and slowly stick one of your fingers in her ass, and don't forget to keep fucking her.

Once both of you are all heated up and fucking like bunnies, it is time for you to increase the tempo of your finger action, and with both holes stuffed at the same time she will be ready to climax on your dick.

While she is riding you, you can also play with her

clit by massaging the upper outer area of her pussy with your thumb – by now this area is very sensitive, so be gentle. You can also reach around her waist and try to insert another finger into her pussy while your dick is inside her, or just play with her clit while you're doing her. Each and every one of those techniques will help to intensify her pleasure level, and it will take you only a little practice to get it right.

Now how about turning her around on her back and grabbing on to her ankles while you fuck her from the front. Doing her on the sofa gives you great control, as you can kneel to fuck her while you relax your legs, or if you want some extra force you can bend over her legs and put your entire weight into your thrust. This will ensure deep and hard penetration and your woman will cry out in appreciation. It gives you the ability to be playful when fucking her – take your cock out with every stroke and rub it against her clit before sticking it back in. Rub it against her asshole, but make sure she isn't afraid you are going anal on her. It takes patience and finesse to get most women to appreciate anal sex. You can even rub your hard dick across her pussy and massage it without penetrating her – there are so many ways to get her more excited and make her come.

Having her lie on her back is an excellent position to fuck, as you can finger her pussy at the same time – remember the clit? Gently massage it. Grab on to her tits and squeeze her nipples while you penetrate her. Lean over to suck her tits or suck on her toes, and run your tongue along her legs – she'll love it…and don't forget to kiss her once in a while; men just forget to do that and it's a shame because it increases the sexual sensation.

How about moving up to her mouth and telling her to suck you in the middle of the session. In the meantime you can stick your fingers in her pussy and play with her while she enjoys your cock in her mouth. It's very sexy to see her suck you with a lustful face. It's also a good way to make sure her pussy is still wet and if not, playing with her clit will get it wet again – remember to watch out for the signs that she is really enjoying it.

Another great position is to close both of her legs and bend them back – make sure you don't ram her knees into her face but that you place them next to her head. Now look at that ass and pussy – isn't it just a marvelous view? Both her pussy and ass are staring back at you and this should get you very aroused. You can now eat her pussy and lick her asshole – make sure to invest some time here, before sticking your dick back in. Do it slowly and deep before you increase your pace – as I pointed out before. In general it is highly recommended to alter the tempo of your penetration rhythms – women can easily get "bored" by a monotonous thrust action when the pussy gets adjusted to the rhythm. Changing the rhythm and force of your thrusts will ensure she can't anticipate the next move.

The same positions can be enjoyed using one of the dining table chairs. Sit down and let your woman mount you and enjoy a wild ride. It's now her turn to take the lead and pleasure you the way she sees fit. She can do it facing you (if she does, tend to her tits, suck them, massage them, bite them gently) or with her ass turned to you. You'll enjoy it either way and you can always choose to lend a hand – I hope that by now you understand what I am referring to. The advantages of chair fucking are that you will penetrate your woman very deeply without having to do much. It's mainly her body weight that ensures you will fill her up all the way.

The living room offers you more options – like the floor. I know sometimes it's not the most comfortable place to fuck – but that's good, it's often the memory of having fucked on the floor that brings even greater pleasure and there are ways to make it comfortable. You can place pillows under her knees while she bends over all the way to expose her ass to you (she will appreciate the gesture). This is one of the best ways to penetrate her very deeply and it's a beautiful site to every ass aficionado. If you opt for this position, make sure your legs are up to it. Strong legs are required to endure a longer fuck session, but it's worth it (especially if you want to make her come). Once in awhile you can lean over her and rest your weight on your arms – but this requires strong arms. What I am telling you here, is that you need to keep in shape if you want to be able to give your woman a good and longer lasting fuck (more on staying in shape and the effects on your love life later in this book, but keep it in mind). If you are less in shape, choose to switch positions more frequently, but make sure you don't interrupt the sexual tension. Too much switching can kill the mood.

The kitchen – a place to fulfill the pleasures of your palate (Oh I do hope you love good food since sex and food go hand in hand) but not only that! It's an excellent place to enjoy a good fuck and it's a new and exciting place for many couples to have sex. Women can be very aroused by the thought of getting fucked in the kitchen – it's a sensual place and just the thought of doing it here, where she may be spending a lot of time preparing meals, can be very satisfying.

Don't be surprised if at one point you see her chopping onions with a big smile on her face. It could be that she is remembering the fuck you had in the kitchen (given that it was fun, of course). I would like you to think of it in terms of changing the scenery so as to change your luck and satisfy your urge. Place her on the kitchen counter or table. You will immediately notice that the height is to your advantage – no more kneeling or acrobatics required to fuck your woman. For us men it is quite comfortable to stand up straight and fuck our women. She can close her legs around your waist and you can grab on to her ass to increase your forceful thrusts. It's a very sensual position and you can kiss passionately while enjoying this position. You can easily press your face between her tits and suck on them to give her some multi-task sex action.

Another fantasy that is easily fulfilled is to fuck your woman while she is preparing food or cooking at the stove. It's up to you to take charge and seek out the opportunities to fulfill your fantasies (and possibly hers too) and to satisfy your urge for hot, raw and dirty sex.

If you are up to it and kinky enough, you can use several kitchen utensils to explore sexual pleasures you might not have been aware of. Many of the kitchen tools can act as substitutes for some of the more commonly used sex toys. I'm going to explore the toy issue in more detail in a chapter on sex toys. Other fantasies worth exploring are mixing food into your sex routine. Smear honey or chocolate syrup on her erogenous zones and enjoy, for example, licking them off her pussy (it will add another dimension to your definition of "eating pussy"). Some of you might remember the movie scene in "9 ½ Weeks." If you don't, you might want to YouTube it to refresh your memory.

More favorite places to fuck in the home are the balcony, terrace or garden. For many of you, it might constitute the first step outside of the protective confinement of your home and you must definitely try it out. Afraid that your neighbors are watching? Who gives a shit – they just envy you and wish they could fuck like you do. For starters you can do it at night when most people are watching TV (this time you are not!) and in the cover of darkness until you are comfortable enough to try it in broad daylight (which gives you an extra kick). Do it on the garden furniture, do it on the lawn or while she holds on to the balustrade – Just Do It! (Makes you wonder what the Nike commercial had in mind with this slogan.)

I hope that by now you understand the deeper meaning of fucking your woman in every room in your home – I mean every room – apart from the kids' room. There are no taboos as this is your home and you and your woman, as a couple, are entitled to let go of your inhibitions. Having sex in all the rooms is a secret you both share and you will occasionally notice that you glance at each other remembering the hot sex or great fuck you both enjoyed at a specific spot. It will pave the way for more sex and it will make your woman see you in a different light. You're the king of the castle and it's time you started acting like it.

COME OUTSIDE

Now that you are the master of your home, the next and bigger step is to leave the privacy of your home and take your sex adventures farther afield. This means stepping out into the open and fucking outside – wherever the opportunity presents itself.

Where to start? There are so many good locations to choose from, I certainly cannot cover all of them. And I am sure that some of you have found great places to enjoy good sex. For many men, even the basics are high hanging fruit that are out of reach. My goal is to hand you a ladder so you can reach those desirable fruits and taste their exotic flavors. When it comes to fucking outside, there are no forbidden fruits. What's allowed and what's not depends solely on your risk level. What I would like to share with you are the basics, mixed with some of the more exotic locations.

To make it easier for you to find your risk level, I have categorized the various locations into three risk levels. This will help you to explore the fun of sex on the go, without the fear of stepping into a situation where you don't know the risk involved. The problem is that if you are constantly worrying about who's going to jump you, it's likely you will have problems maintaining your hard-on and then all your good intentions will be wasted. The last thing we want is for your dick to stay down – no, no, your woman won't appreciate that, especially now that she is anticipating some fun. You have surprised her and convinced her to take down her panties in public, so you have to step up to the plate and at least make it to first base – a home run is, of course, better, but you don't want to take on too much on your first away game. Once you get more familiar with the concept of sex in public, you will gain the confidence to deflect your fears and increase your risk level so as to attain even more rewarding sex rushes.

Yeah – fucking your woman in public will give you a never-before-experienced sex rush. It's the most exhilarating, liberating and satisfying sex that you'll experience. In fact, some men I know have become addicted to this rush and continually seek new and riskier ways to satisfy their need. But keep in mind that everything should be experienced in good measure – this is true of everything we consume and certainly true for our thirst to experience exciting sex. Sex can easily turn into an addiction. As you probably know, sex releases all kinds of happy drugs (endorphins) in your brain, and we can easily become endorphin junkies that constantly seek out the next ejaculation to release those endorphins. This is especially true when we combine it with an adrenalin rush, which is induced by challenging ourselves to engage in more daunting sex situations that aim to top the last sensation we experienced.

Don't misunderstand me – I want you to go outside and enjoy sex; just don't make it the rule to fuck outside – your home should always remain your preferred choice. It's there that you and your woman share a unique intimacy that you continuously need to nourish and cherish.

Risk level 1:

This level is fairly safe. The risk of getting caught in the act is relatively low. Locations with this risk level are:

Public restrooms – You and your woman can easily enter the restroom when no one is watching. You have ensured privacy (just don't forget to lock the door and make sure it is a closed off restroom and not one of those stalls inviting every passerby to stop by for a private show). You should also make sure your woman is not a screamer and that you don't groan like a pig when you're getting sucked off or fucking your woman. Suppressing your moans and groans can result in an elevated pleasure level, as much of the otherwise released tension is sort of bottled up, which raises the overall sensation.

The car – The car is a fairly safe playground, and the risk level of car sex depends, of course, on the spot you pick to take out your dick. A secluded location like the woods, the park, a parking garage, or a small street are ideal to enjoy good sex – especially if you do it during night hours when most people are sound asleep. The only person likely to take you by surprise is someone walking his dog. Nonetheless, be prepared for a little acrobatics to master the tight space (unless you are the owner of a luxury sedan), but in my experience fucking in a tight space can ignite your imagination and a big car is just too similar to your sofa. The same, of course, can be said of vans, which are nothing other than small bedrooms on wheels. If you live in an area that offers the choice of breathtaking viewpoints, then you should make sure to stop by for a car fuck. The mixed experience of looking at some of nature's most beautiful scenery and fucking your woman will last for a lifetime.

Hotel room – Of course you will say: So? And I will reply: Why aren't you doing it then? Men should once in a while surprise their woman by taking her to a nice hotel for a naughty bed session. This can either happen during lunch break or after a romantic dinner. In the latter case, your woman will very much appreciate a change in scenery rather than continuing home to complete the routine of fucking you after a great night out. For any men that haven't thought of this or are too stingy to pay up, I'm telling you that it can be very rewarding. Hotel rooms get us to do things we normally refrain from doing, and the only explanation I have is that it happens because we are not at home. Domestic rules and routine fucking patterns do not apply in hotel rooms. Your fantasies can run wild and you can throw your inhibitions overboard.

However, make sure to take your woman to a nice hotel (it should at least be a 4-star and have some style). It tells her that you are investing in her and that you want to pamper her as much as you can. Men with the monetary means should opt for a hotel in their affordable price range; your good idea can backfire if you take her to an establishment that is beneath your salary level. And you should consider ordering room service (champagne is good), perhaps ordering a porn flick on the pay-per-view channel, and possibly indulging in the mini bar. Your woman will return your generosity with uninhibited and often surprising sex acts. Be prepared to experience some of the kinky stuff you've always wanted to try out at home but couldn't because your woman brushed you off.

Elevator – Elevators are relatively safe; just watch out for cameras that might have been installed for security reasons. Especially elevators in public places such as office buildings, department stores and residential buildings (except for your own apartment building) are great places to have kinky sex. Hit the stop button and don't waste time getting right down to it. This falls into the category of quickies. It's hard, fast and uninhibited sex to satisfy your urge. Do it any way you want, just do it fast. You never know how long it will take for the security guard or doorman on duty to call the janitor or maintenance crew to get you out. By then you should have zipped up your dick and your lady should have rearranged her skirt and straightened her blouse. You can increase the sensation by a lot if you do it in one of the glass elevators with a breathtaking view of the city skyline – just make sure you are on one of the upper floors when you hit the stop button – unless you don't care if people might be watching you from below or from the opposite building.

Risk level 2:
This level is somewhat risky as the chance of someone walking in on you is greater. Locations with this risk level are:

Dining table – Have you ever been jerked off by your woman while sitting at the table and conversing with the people around you? It takes great self control to maintain an indifferent posture and go on as if nothing is happening – especially if the stroking and rubbing of your cock intensifies and you are about to ejaculate. Your woman has to be as discrete as you, of course, and master the art of jerking you off without an over-extensive and obvious hand movement. The reward is gratifying and very bonding. Of course you can return the favor and play with your woman's pussy until she reaches her orgasm. Again, just make sure to mainly use your fingers and keep your arm from moving around. Enjoy the feeling when she tightens her thighs around your hand, nearly crushing it, as she is about to come. And by the way, make sure you have a napkin handy to clean up the sperm residue before you zip up your dick. It can be very embarrassing having sperm on your pants when you get up from the table.

Movie theater – Again, a good place for some frivolous hand spiel. Make sure to go to a daytime screening as the theater will be mostly empty. Then chose a seat location that gives you the privacy you need – top or bottom rows and far enough from the entrance. Depending on how crowded the theater is and how far you are willing to go, you can start off with first base action and then move on to fill all the bases. Once you are 15-20 minutes into the movie, the chances of late comers walking into the theater and seating themselves near you are low and you will be fairly safe with the seats you have chosen. Some couples go all the way and lie between the rows and fuck – hopefully you can free yourself one day to join their ranks. You can be sure that no matter how bad the movie was, you will think it should have been nominated for an Oscar.

The ocean – By this I refer to a fuck in the water while people are standing around you or can see you from the beach. Just like with the dining table hand action, you have to be able to remain calm and collected when you are doing it. The thrusting motion has to be slow and inconspicuous and you can try to sync it with the movement of the waves. Couples (the loving ones) tend to hold each other close in the water and kiss. Everyone envies couples on vacation that are able to express their affection for each other publicly, but their envy would be even greater if they were able to see below the water line and find out that you and your woman are engaged in a sexual encounter.

There are two ways to do it without drawing too much attention. The first one is from behind, while you are embracing her from behind and the second one is to do it facing each other while she closes her legs around your waist. The great thing is that the water carries most of the body weight and you can simply grab on to our woman's ass if she decides to mount you. There is no need to take off your bathing suit, and women can easily shift their bathing suit to the side to let you penetrate their pussy. As all the action happens below the waterline you can also play with her pussy before the fuck or while you're fucking her. The more courageous dare to take off their suits, but make sure to keep at least one leg in your suit as it can be embarrassing to have to call for someone to throw you a towel.

Airplane lavatory – For some reason, many men fantasize about joining the Mile High Club, i.e., having sex in the lavatory of an airplane. Well...while it is quite satisfying to reduce the pressure (of course I am not referring to the sensation in your ears caused by cabin pressure) that has built up on a long haul flight, you have to understand that it's not one of the more comfortable fucks. It's very similar to fucking in the cramped space of a sports car. There is simply not much room to maneuver. Still, if the urge is great and the opportunity presents itself (meaning your woman is in the mood to try out something new) to fulfill one of your sexual fantasies – then go for it.

Not every plane provides you with the opportunity to simply step into the lavatory with your woman. There are typically many watchful eyes and the flight attendant may knock on the door to disrupt whatever you are doing. That's why I am referring to long haul flights as they usually involve large aircraft with several lavatories.

You should wait for the night time, when the cabin lights are out and most of the passengers are either asleep or busy watching a movie. This will present you with the opportunity to follow your woman to the lavatory and step into the cabin undetected. Of course you should try to keep your noise level to a minimum, so as not to attract unwanted attention.

The tricky part is getting out of the lavatory without being confronted by passengers waiting in line. A quick glimpse through the slit of the door can tell you if the coast is clear and if not you simply shut the door as if you have to continue your business. Waiting for the night time will greatly reduce the chances of having to confront waiting passengers.

Fitting room – Here is another unfulfilled fantasy for many men and it's not that difficult to fulfill, especially if the fitting room is fitted with a door and a lock. The only thing you have to do is wait for the right moment when the sales assistant is occupied and then step into the room with your woman. It even works when the aisle of the fitting rooms is packed with people trying on clothes or critiquing outfits – there are always friends or family or men who are waiting outside the door for the next display of garments. Most of the people are just too busy to notice if you disappear, and if they do notice, they are too naïve to believe that you're about to fuck your woman.

Once again I cannot stress the fact enough that you will have to be the master of your voices and noises. Since you are in a confined environment, every groan and moan will be heard, and if you have problems suppressing them, my tip is to stuff a T-shirt or another piece of clothing into your mouth and bite on it.

If you are confident enough to try this stunt in a fitting room with curtains, then this falls into the level 3 category. Just think of how many times you have been caught in your underwear while trying on clothes because someone peeked through the curtains to see if the fitting room was vacant. Imagine the expression on their face if they saw you taking your woman from behind or if they saw your woman riding you while you were sitting on a chair (of course not every fitting room offers the comfort of a chair). However, the idea of someone walking in at any minute and catching you in the middle of a fuck or blow job can be exhilarating and for sure it will intensify the experience. You and your woman will look back many times on the day that you both stepped into a fitting room and fucked while people were waiting in line for you to come out. For sure you will remember their questioning and surprised faces when you both stepped out with a radiant look on your face.

Risk level 3:

This level is risky to very risky. In my opinion, it provides the greatest sexual reward, but it requires either strong nerves (So what?) or a high level of indifference (I don't give a shit) in case you are caught with your pants down or better. You should build up your confidence level before exploring these exhilarating and adrenalin packed (s)e(x)scapades.

The beach – Ahh yes. This is a nice one and is not to be confused with sex in the ocean as mentioned earlier. This refers to fucking on the beach, where one is likely to meet people strolling along the shoreline to take in the magnificent view of a sunlit white beach or taking a romantic walk under a starlit sky. Some of you might be that lucky to be in a location that offers secluded beaches during the day time. Honestly, I don't see any sexual pleasure in ruining the scenery by fucking my woman in front of an audience (this is really hard core stuff).

There are, however, some vacation spots on earth that provide you with the opportunity to take a boat and sail out to a small deserted island or drive to a secluded beach to fulfill a truly wonderful sexual fantasy. Men and women alike are very open to engaging in a hot fuck scene on the beach as long as they believe they are alone. So why is this level 3? Because you never know if you are alone or if someone is watching you through a set of high-powered binoculars. At any point someone could walk up and greet you with a broad grin, while you are doing your woman. There are not many places you can hide if this happens.

As for beach sex during the night hours – luckily there are many more opportunities to realize a beach fuck and this definitely doesn't imply that you need to be on a secluded beach. The idea is to take cover in the darkness and stay undetected while you fuck. However, don't be mistaken; there is a 50% chance that someone will notice what's going on. But the great thing about being on vacation is that no one really cares. Besides, most of the people you meet on your holiday you'll never see again in your life. So why the fuck should you care about what stran-gers think of you? Quickly get over your embarrassment and enjoy whatever it is you're doing. You can take cover in the tree line while overseeing the beach, you can do it on the lifeguard tower, or you can do it on one of the beach chairs. You can even use the beach chairs to build yourself a protective screen. If you believe that you're on a quiet strip of beach and your confidence is all boosted up by the higher than normal alcohol level – then go for it. It's not always necessary to get bare naked – removing your pants is more than sufficient to guide your dick into the pussy – and some of you may want to leave your pants on, in case you need to pull them up quickly. The only thing I want to remind you of is that you are at the beach and that means lots of sand. So be extra careful that dick and pussy do not get in contact with the sand or you'll have a rather hurtful experience.

Despite potential interruptions, I strongly suggest you overcome any reservations you might have and talk your woman into fucking you on the beach. It's one of the moments you will both cherish for the rest of your lives and memories of this kind are hard to come by. Too often these opportunities are left unexploited and that can leave behind a bitter taste. Unfortunately for many couples, the opportunity for a secluded-island-beach-fuck might present itself only once in a lifetime and what a waste not to act upon it. Don't be one of those sissies that for some idiotic reason missed out on having great sex on the beach with his woman.

Swimming pool – Here we have to differ between a public pool and a private pool. The one I am referring to is the public pool. The private pool belongs in the level 1 category. Whereas the public pool is more exciting, the private pool gives you the opportunity to try out great things.

Let's start with the public pool. It is very similar to the ocean fuck, but with one big difference. The water here is clear and people are standing much closer. Still, to the confident lovers among the male sex it doesn't present an obstacle. We will not be denied a chance to fuck our women only because we are in the middle of a pool surrounded by a shouting and joyous crowd. The right way is to pick a corner and move to a water depth where we can stand. Just like in the ocean you can chose from two comfortable positions. I'm sure you'll like it once you've tried it out. Men...make sure your hard-on is down before you exit the pool. For God's sake, there are kids around and we wouldn't want them asking their moms why you are showing off your tent.

Fucking in a private pool (if you own one, it falls into the chapter on fucking everywhere in your house) – possibly at your friend's house, your boss's house or in the private pool of your hotel room – can be very rewarding. There are lots of positions you can try out – for example, sitting your woman on the edge of the pool and burying your face between her widespread legs or having her return the favor by sucking you off while you sit on the pool edge. Ever had your dick sucked under water? Make sure your woman takes a deep breath before going scuba on you. There is something very sensual about doing it naked in the pool. It's like the entire pool transforms into a huge playground, and with gravity to your advantage, you can easily engage in sexual positions that are difficult to achieve on dry land.

The park – It's a nice place to take your woman after a date and seduce her into fucking you right where you are. There are lots of great places you can choose from – on the grass, on a park bench, or on the swing at the playground (very nice indeed). Again, your risk factor of being caught depends on the hour you choose for your adventure. The later the hour, the more unlikely it will be for a dog owner to accidentally drop in for a late night porn session. Pick a warm night and clear skies for a tête-à-tête to improve your chances of success. Most women will not pull down their pants when it's cold outside, and if you haven't understood by now, I'll repeat that we can't have our women be distracted when we are about to fuck them.

Jacuzzi – By now you understand that sexual acts of pleasure are not limited to fucking when you are alone. There is as much pleasure in foreplay and hand spiel as there is in the actual fuck itself. So did you ever get a hand-job while sitting in a bubbling hot tub with people sitting around you and looking right at you? Quite liberating, I assure you. As long as the bubbles are blurring the view under water, it's quite safe to try it out. Just be careful to keep your suits on as they will otherwise float to the surface and that's a bummer (yes, yes, this can happen very easily). The great thing about a hot tub is that you can easily engage in a reciprocal hand spiel. The big challenge will be for you to keep an inconspicuous facial expression while your woman is stroking your hard cock. Make sure not to move around too much as this will give you away. This type of hand treatment will certainly shed a different light on the "hot" in hot tub.

I could go on for pages and pages, but this is not a guide to the 100 best sex locations. I just want you to open your mind when you think of sex locations and it doesn't always have to be the act of fucking that will guarantee you the pleasure you are seeking. A lot of the fun stuff definitely lies in the foreplay category and the great pleasure you experience is a result of the spontaneity and the unexpected or unusual location for sexual acts. What I'd like you to do is write down all the locations you fantasize about and where you wish you could enjoy sex with your woman – don't be shy and think of your dirtiest fantasies (Where and how would you like to fuck your woman?).

I assure you that someone before you has had the same dirty thoughts, or even better, has realized these wishes already – so there is no reason to feel ashamed or uncomfortable. As a test of your conviction to change your sex life and improve the relationship with your woman, I'd like you to realize one of the top three fantasies within the next seven days. Make it your personal goal to cross out one of the top three sex locations on your list. You will be amazed at the liberating feeling you experience once you achieve this goal. The next step is to cross out two more of your top ten locations by the end of the month. You will be challenged to be creative and to be ambitious about creating the situations that will allow you to realize your fantasies. After you accomplish several of your sexual fantasies, you will start to notice a different expression on your woman's face when she looks at you. What she will be thinking is: "Where the fuck was this man hiding all the time?"

This doesn't mean that you will stop what you have put into motion. Your goal is to cross off all of your I-would-like-to-fuck-my-woman-at locations. Now that your mind and body have conquered your fears, you will see how easy it becomes to dream up new and exciting places to have sex. Essentially every location where you and your woman are together becomes a potential location for having sex of any kind – finger, suck, eat, stroke and fuck.

Enjoy!

PUSH-UPS, SIT-UPS, SEX-UP

Did you ever wonder if Sex and Sport are related? They sure are. Sex is definitely a high-impact aerobic discipline and as such requires you to be in good shape if you want to excel at it. In order for you to please your woman, you must take care of your body from a physical and esthetic standpoint. Physical, because you want to be able to pull an all-nighter or at least a longer fuck session that ensures your woman reaches her orgasm. Esthetic, because our women will like us better with several pounds less around our waists.

Don't mistake this for ripped abs and bulging pecs; being in shape doesn't require you to look like an Adonis. A few pounds less and a flat stomach will get the proper attention of your woman. The mere fact that she sees you move your ass to get into shape and then maintain it will secure her admiration. If it also translates into better, longer and harder sex, so much the better. Especially once we men get older we have to do more to keep the excess pounds from building up and turning the most fun activity in the world into a strenuous, short-of-breath and dangerous endeavor.

As long as we are young, our heart will play along with the alcohol, smoking, drugs and fatty foods we throw at it and we will still be able to perform at full throttle. The older we get, the more careful we have to be about indulging in all the vices, and although I can do without the alcohol, smoking, drugs and fatty foods, I certainly don't want to miss out on fucking my woman. You men must understand that there is always a kind of vicious cycle out there that is trying to capture us and lure us into giving up on sex and replacing it with the aforementioned vices. Don't let yourself get drawn into this cycle, and if you already have, then it's about time to break out. All the vices are nothing but poor substitutes for the best drug in the world – sex.

Earlier in the book I mentioned that good sex is dependent on certain muscle groups that are more dominant in sexual workouts. I am referring to your leg and butt muscles, and your abs, waist and arms. Each of these muscle groups should be strengthened in your exercise routine and you will notice the results when you try out different positions or ones you thought you couldn't maintain long enough for your woman to enjoy them properly. Another plus from getting in shape is the impact on your mental state. Regular workouts will drastically improve your libido and replace feelings of tiredness with energetic and enthusiastic spontaneity for sex, which is excellent for your health in general. Just in case you didn't know, men with a healthy sex life (this implies meaningful sex with your woman and not random fucking) have a lesser chance of falling victim to various heart diseases. Furthermore, if your heart is used to aerobic exercise, it is likely not to fail in times of strenuous and enduring sex games. Therefore, my fellow men, exercise, exercise, exercise, and your sexual gratification will be enormous.

Be prepared if your woman becomes jealous of your sudden exercise routines, as it can make you look better than she does, which can lead to an upset in the natural balance of a relationship. She might be intimidated by the new you, especially if she doesn't find the time to work out as regularly as you do. If your woman mentions to you that she feels chubby, fat or undesirable, you must calm her with encouraging words and let her know that she is just exaggerating and that she's the woman you desire to be with. Let her know that she still gives you a hard-on when you see her naked, and be sensitive about telling her to work out a little more or eat a little less.

In case you are not good with words, just shut your mouth and stick to the basics, which are "Honey, I love everything about you and you are still that sexy bitch that gives me a hard-on." Just be genuinely sincere when you talk to your woman, as she will easily know if you feed her crap. If your situation permits it, you can offer to exercise together and enjoy the mutual benefits of getting into shape and improving your sex life.

FOREPLAY VS. FOUL PLAY

I promised you a detailed section on foreplay, so here we go. This is definitely my favorite subject and for some reason the majority of men simply don't understand that it's the most important sexual component for women. It is even more important than fucking itself. Good foreplay prepares your woman physically and mentally for the fuck and it will make her reach levels of satisfaction and excitement that your dick will never achieve on its own. Even if you are fortunate enough to be exceptionally well hung (which is the exception to the rule), good foreplay will more than compensate for the average Joe's cock size (More on the truth about large cocks in the subsequent chapter).

Let me put it this way: foreplay generates the natural lubricant your woman needs to enjoy longer, harder and more exciting sex. It helps your woman to relax and it puts her mind at rest, setting aside all the distracting thoughts in her head that can ruin a great fuck. It helps your woman to close the gap between your steep and fast orgasm curve and her long and slow orgasm curve. It is imperative that you understand how important it is to sync between the male and female sexual timeline, particularly if you want to reach a simultaneous (the most gratifying) orgasm with your woman. Are you one of those men that don't even bother to touch your woman's pussy and your only definition of sex is to stick your cock into her pussy and rub it (because that's exactly what you're doing) until you spurt off? Shame on you, you egotistical bastard! And you have no idea what you're missing.

So what's good foreplay and what do women like? Well it starts with kissing. Yes, yes, kissing is foreplay – What? You didn't know? Not to be confused with the tongue-deep-in-her-mouth kiss, I am referring to the gentle and sensual kiss, which then builds up to a passionate lock of your lips with the occasional tongue-shake. Remember the first-ever kiss you and your woman had? This is the type of kiss you should start with. I am quite sure you didn't shove tongue down her throat the instant you started kissing; hopefully you progressed slowly and gently, until you eventually found yourselves engaged in a passionate exchange of fluids. This is what you're aiming for. Unfortunately men often tend to neglect the very basic act of sharing affection with their woman, which is kissing. So here is the rule – every fuck (or almost every one) starts with kissing, and a famous movie quote describes it perfectly: "I'd like to get kissed before

I get fucked."

Having established that, let's move on. There are severallevels of foreplay and each one provides a higher level of sexual intensity and prepares your woman for the next step in the sexual encounter. The next level is caressing your woman when she is still dressed. Embrace your woman and press her close to you. Move your hands across her entire body. Cover all her parts, star-ting from her neck down to the back and ass. Make your hands felt and don't just wipe them along her body. Increase the hand pressure as you kiss and make your intentions felt. By now your cock is already hard and your woman knows where this is heading. Invest several minutes caressing her back before you hands come to rest on her ass. Massage her ass gently and increase the pressure of your hands and fingers moving them in and out between her ass cheeks. Once in a while grab on to the cheeks and release them. Keep your woman pressed close to your body so she can feel your hard-on. This definitely signals to her that you are turned on by her assets.

Now tend to her front parts. I like to move my hands between the ass and pussy area. Gently move your hands between her legs and squeeze the crotch area. Rub your hands gently between her legs – remember to keep your hands out of her pants. Feel her tits, squeeze them gently, feel the roundness of them and try to find the nipples through all the layers of clothing and massage them between your fingers. Don't hurt her! This can ruin the entire setup and rip her out of her "well, why not?" state of mind.

Don't give her any reason or excuse to reject you. Kiss her neck and earlobes – What? You thought you were passed kissing? Wrong! Kissing goes on throughout the foreplay phase, although at some point it's of secondary importance.

Once your woman reciprocates your crotch massage by massaging the hard-on in your pants, it's time for you to move your hands into her pants. Try something new and don't open the button to her pants or undo the zipper. Shove your hand into her pants, but don't reach under her panties. To your woman it indicates that you have time – and good things (like sex) take time. Play with and massage her pussy through her panties until you can feel the pussy juices wetting the panties. Try to hold your horses and not stick your finger in her pussy for as long as possible. Keep playing – occasionally move the panties to the side to feel her pussy, pretending to have touched the area accidentally and then move your finger above the panties to continue the massage.

You can wait for the panties to be soaked or very wet before you decide to touch her flesh. It's really not necessary to stick your finger right away into her pussy; there are still a lot of things you can do before that. One of the most sensitive parts of a woman's pussy is not inside her pussy (contrary to the G-spot), but rather at the upper tip of her pussy lips – and it's the clitoris or clit! It's time you get acquainted with this tiny and very important female organ that is responsible for many of your woman's orgasms. The trained man will know to carefully tend to the clit and rub it very gently and slowly – the more gentle and slow you are, the more your woman will enjoy it. Yes, it is in complete contrast to the male understanding of sex, which is mostly about fast and hard action. Many women do not know how to explain to their men what it is they need them to do – either they have never experienced it or they are too shy or afraid to tell them – and therefore I want you to know what to do – gently and slowly. The more patience you show and the gentler you are to your woman, the more she is going to be surprised and the more she is going to appreciate what you are doing to her.

The next step is to reach under her shirt and feel her naked breasts. The same technique applies here. If you can play with her tits and nipples while her bra stays on, it will send the right message, which is that you are patient enough and not an inconsiderate and wild animal as many women believe men to be. Once you decide to unbutton her shirt, keep it on and start to kiss her tits. Again, contrary to what many men think, it's not only the nipples that get your woman aroused, it's the tissue around the nipple and the entire breast area that, when touched and kissed, get her to moan with pleasure. To many women, kissing and caressing these areas can be more gratifying than sucking the nipple, as these may be areas that you have unknowingly neglected all those years. Not anymore!

How about kneeling down in front of her and kissing her naked tummy. The lower tummy area of your woman is a pleasure zone when gently kissed. Kiss her crotch – ever kissed a dressed crotch? Yeah! Women find it sexy. I also like to turn my woman around and reach from behind into her pants to play with her pussy and also massage her tits. Playing with her while you stand behind her gives you better control of your hands, which can be more comfortable for both of you. By now, she should be rubbing her ass against your hard cock, which is the signal you have been waiting for.

What's next? Getting her out of her clothes. You, on the other hand, stay dressed; your cock is going nowhere for now. The location for the sex act is irrelevant, by now you already know that I want you to do it in every room at home and at any location you can think of. What's important now is to wait as long as possible before you stick your cock in your woman's pussy. I don't care how wet she is or if she is telling you to fuck her – you simply don't. Now it is time for extensive finger play and pussy eating. Your goal is to make your woman come at least twice without sticking your cock into one of her love holes. The art of foreplay is to feel your woman and get her to reach one or several peaks way before you start to fuck her; this way you don't have to feel bad if your woman doesn't come during the actual fuck. It can dissolve any pressure you might feel to make your woman come when you fuck her and remove any performance anxiety you might struggle with. On the other hand, your woman will be so aroused that her chances of coming again when you fuck her are high, and she will experience increased pleasure and excitement when you penetrate her.

Fingering your woman's pussy is not as easy as you may think. It's a mixture of different finger techniques and applied levels of pressure that ensure your woman receives the special treatment she seeks and deserves. If you haven't understood it by now, please let me repeat – gently, gently and gently. Your woman's pussy is very different from your cock. Whereas your best friend mostly prefers rougher treatment, your woman's pussy needs to be pampered before it can be exposed to heavy pounding. You just cannot go from 0 to 60 without the risk of causing your woman pain, and that is totally unacceptable.

You have to make sure your woman is physically ready – in plain words, that her pussy is wet, aroused, swollen and expanded enough to welcome your dick. I suggest you start using your middle finger to gently stroke the area between her pussy lips without penetrating her. Focus on the area above the vaginal opening where the clit is located. Apply a slow, circular and one-directional finger motion. Try to keep the same tempo, and stick with the same direction, as women need longer to build up their excitement level. Changing either the tempo or direction of your circling motion or applying too much pressure will disturb your woman's ability to focus on her growing arousal. You can play with her pussy lips, squeezing them gently between your thumb and index finger, and you can softly pull at them to further intensify the excitement.

Another good technique is to rub her pussy gently with your flat hand and to reach down to her asshole and touch it. If your woman is wet, really wet, then you are doing it right. However, the time to fuck has not arrived yet...patience, patience. Now I'd like you to touch her inner thighs. Have you ever noticed that this is the area with the softest skin? Caress her inner thighs on both legs, and when you switch, make sure to slide your hand over her pussy. It is good to extend your stroke down to the feet and back up to the thigh area. It shows your woman that her entire body is important to you and not only her pussy, tits and ass. If you are capable, try to work several of her erogenous areas simultaneously. Play gently with her pussy, while the other hand tends to her tits. Kiss her passionately while your hands explore her entire body, with the occasional stopover at her wet pussy. Multi-tasking will increase your woman's excitement level and can send your woman's erogenous zones into overdrive.

For many men tending to more than one female sex organ at a time constitutes a difficult task. We men are naturally handicapped when it comes to concentrating on more than one task simultaneously. However, I cannot emphasize it enough: we have to work on mastering the art of multi-tasking if we want to better please our women.

Turn you woman around so she lies on her stomach and marvel at the ass staring back at you. Start to massage her ass, softly at first, and then steadily increase the pressure, as you continue to massage and squeeze her butt cheeks. Your woman's ass is not as sensitive as her pussy, and at one point you should massage it firmly, spreading her ass cheeks apart in a pushing circular motion. The ass can take some punishment and it's okay if you want to spank it. Just try it without leaving your fingerprints on her ass – especially if you haven't done it before. Start softly, and depending on her reaction increase the power of your smacks on her ass. You will be amazed at how many women actually fancy being spanked on the ass (some are even hard core and like it when you slap their tits). Who knows, you might both suddenly realize that you are fond of a little punishment and that all that was missing to spice up your sex life was a step into the world of S&M and bondage.

When you massage her ass, you should make sure her pussy opens every time you spread her ass apart. You can even keep her ass spread open for a few seconds to look at her gaping holes. The sight will arouse you, and your woman will be aroused by the feeling of her wide open pussy.

Place your hands and fingers close to her holes, but don't touch them. It's the close proximity of your fingers to her pussy and asshole that increases her arousal and makes her wonder when you finally will touch or finger them. Caress her back and neckline and return to the roundness of her ass. Always try to apply a mixture of gentle and rough play. Kiss her ass cheeks from time to time to let her know how much you love to work her ass. Then let her kneel and present her ass to you. Touch her pussy and slide your hand across her pussy lips, while your other hand is holding on to her ass (spank if you want). You can now move behind her into a doggy style position and rub your hard cock against her pussy lips, but don't penetrate her. Think of your cock like a big finger that is teasing your woman's pussy. Rub it between her pussy lips and press it against her clit, then use the tip of your cock to massage her clit. You can even place your cock between her ass cheeks and rub it along her asshole. Then of course you can turn her around and rub your cock on her tits, or go for a full titty fuck if that's your thing. There is no need for your woman to be equipped with double Ds to enjoy it; it is the idea that counts and women with smaller tits will appreciate it if you think of their tits in ways that want to make you rub your cock on them. You can once again make use of the tip of your cock to play with her nipples and get them all hard.

Now it's time to stick your fingers in her wet pussy. Start with one finger. If you are lying next to her, the best finger to start with is your middle finger as it is the longest and is flanked by your other fingers, which you can press against your woman's pussy when your middle finger is all the way inside her. The exerted pressure on the surrounding pussy area is important and provides additional pleasure that shouldn't be ignored. You should bend your finger once it is in the pussy, as if you would like to pierce it from the inside through her stomach – depending on how deep you go, you can hit the G-spot. Despite repeating myself, I remind you once again how important it is for you to know what and where the G-spot is. The G-spot, to the still ignorant among the male readership, is the internal equivalent of the externally situated clit. However, as rewarding and pleasurable a clit-induced orgasm can be, it is nothing compared to the G-spot-triggered orgasm supported by a squirting pussy.

Move your finger all around the inside of her pussy and explore all the areas inside her. The next step is to insert your index finger and do a tandem finger job on her pussy. This will stretch her pussy and give you more strength with each of your strokes. Attention please…Place your thumb on her clit, while your fingers are inside in her pussy. Let your thump move in a circular motion, first gently and then stronger. This will intensify your finger technique immensely and greatly increase your woman's pleasure and arousal.

By the way – are your listening to your woman? Are you continuing to watch out for the signals? Remember your woman will tell you through her body language if she likes what you're doing or if you should increase or soften your finger exercise. Some women possess a very flexible pussy and you should find out just how flexible it is by inserting another finger. The next finger to insert is the ring finger. Make sure to play a little with her pussy, so as to stretch it further, before inserting another finger, your pinkie. Did you even know that your woman was able and ready to have four fingers in her pussy at the same time and have you ever hand fucked her before? Will she also take the entire hand? You will be amazed at how many women do, if they are aroused enough and if you have prepared the pussy well.

 A great technique that will bring your woman to new levels of ecstasy is fingering her with your thumb. Only your thumb! Slide it in and out and use your freed up fingers to play with her asshole. Be careful – not every woman knows how to take it, so be careful when sticking a finger up her ass. Often it is enough to just play with her asshole. Now increase the speed of your hand, using your thumb to reach deep into her pussy hole. Continuously increase the speed of your hand, and at some point you should be pumping your hand so hard and fast that you think you might be hurting your woman – but you are not! By now she is so wet and ready to pop, and if you do it right you can get her to squirt. It's all in the thumb, I'm telling you! It works even better when she is kneeling and you insert your thumb from behind into her pussy (recall the previous chapter on the Fountain of Joy). You can kneel or stand at her side, which will give you better control of your hand motion and make it easier for you to increase the speed.

Your woman will start to scream and push as you increase your pumping action; it is now crucial that you learn how far you can go. Your woman might already be coming (maybe even more than once), but you have to continue your fast and wild thumb ride if you want her to come in ways she has never experienced before. The ultimate goal, of course, is to get your woman to spurt, and if she does, it might be the first time for either one or both of you. The important thing to remember is not to be taken aback by what's happening. It's a natural reaction to an overstimulation of your woman's sex organs, in particular the G-spot.

You can pride yourself if you manage to give you woman this gift of pleasure and you can be sure that she will appreciate you more for having let her experience an explosive orgasm. From this point forward she will look differently at orgasms and it will be your achievement. The only reason I am repetitive on this subject is because I believe it is very important for men to know how to get their women to squirt. It is a woman's ultimate orgasm, and mastering the art of getting your women to squirt will gain you a huge sexual advantage. Your woman will be able to experience, with you and by you, the most fantastic orgasms, which removes most of the performance pressure from the equation. You will now be in the position to shoot your load whenever you need to, and without ruining the win-win scenario.

Finger techniques, as we now understand, are fun and important, but for many women getting their pussy eaten is king. If there is one thing women really like, it is to get their pussy licked the right way. There is a softness only your tongue can achieve and you can lick a pussy for an hour without your woman getting fed up with it. Eating pussy is a mixture of softness and firmness, and you need to alternate between both to extend the mutual pleasure (yeah, for me it's the best thing about sex, next to a squirting pussy) for as long as possible, until you simply have the uncontrollable urge to fuck your woman hard. The longer you can keep yourself from jumping her, the better for both of you. There is no better way to get your woman excited and horny as hell. For many women, getting their pussy eaten is the highlight of the fuck session, and if you get your woman to come when your face is buried between her legs (and they can easily come more than once on your face), then the physical fuck itself becomes less important. She will be more relaxed (of course!) and more open to accept your dick in ways she might otherwise reject. It's like an unspoken proposal to return the favor for making her come all over your face.

There are a lot of techniques you should know and master when you lick your woman's pussy. You also need to have a better understanding of your woman's vagina and what really arouses here. This knowledge will help you to perform better when your tongue is exploring her pink flesh. Pussy eating can and should be combined with finger techniques for elevated levels of pleasure, but let's focus first on the licking. I like to differ between two main positions – woman on her back and woman with her ass facing you. Each position provides a myriad of options, but there are different nuances and techniques you should apply. Let's start with the more common female position where your woman lies on her back to reveal her juicy pussy to you by spreading her legs. If your woman is shy about getting her pussy licked, or she has never been licked by you before, because either you were appalled by the thought or she is against any form of fellatio, then it's up to you to reveal to her that until now she was possibly missing out on the best part of sex.

Tell her, with assurance in your voice, to lie down and spread her legs as you are going to lick her pussy. If she responds with a questioning face, repeat your request and help her to find a comfortable position. Once you get down to it, any resistance she might have in the beginning will dissolve with the first shivers of pleasure running up her spine. Start with kissing her pussy lips and running your tongue across her lips. Apply an upward lick motion to get her used to what's coming her way. Kiss the inner sides of her thighs and the area around her pussy as well. Use one or both of your hands to spread her pussy lips and reveal the pink flesh. Once you start burying your face between her legs, take in the smell of her pussy. The sweet smell of her pussy juice works like a pheromone that will get you all horny, making you enjoy every bit of it. When you are licking your woman's pussy, try to imagine you are engaged in a tender kiss. The gentler you are and the more playful you are with your tongue, the more your woman is going to enjoy it.

Remember that you are putting your ego aside at this point and focusing all your attention on satisfying your woman's needs (although I enjoy pussy licking as much as my woman – okay, nearly as much). Look at it this way, when your woman sucks your cock, you are the main beneficiary, and you should give her the same level of pleasure.

Go on now and suck her pussy lips – careful, you don't want to suck them too hard. You can even gently bite them; everything is allowed that gives her pleasure and you can easily know if it is by listening to her and watching out for the right signals. Take one finger and stick it in her pussy while you continue to lick her clit – be ready for a pleasurable moan. Push your finger deep down her hole and turn and twist it to reach the far end of her pussy. The idea is to combine the hand and lick techniques for extended satisfaction. Insert two, three, four and all fingers, if her pussy can handle it and as long as she is not hurting. If you do it right, she will explode in your face.

Ever had a woman come on your face? It's about time.

Some women feel ashamed if it happens, but you should encourage her to come over your face. It will remove another inhibition and increase your trust for each other. When you feel that she is coming, don't stop licking her pussy, hold on to her waist, legs or ass to keep your face buried deep in her pussy and lick, lick, lick. She will bend and moan and (hopefully) shout as she comes all over your face. If you do it right she will easily come more than once. At some point, when she has had one or several orgasms, you have to let her go so she can relax a little. Don't let her get off the peak – that's important now. Put her in the position in which you want to fuck her and just do it. Your woman is now in the orgasmic zone and she will easily come when you fuck her, so take advantage of her heightened arousal and hit the ball out of the park.

As I said earlier, I like to differ between front and back pussy licking. Having your woman on all fours presenting her ass to you is different when it comes to licking. The basic techniques are the same, but you can position yourself below her pussy and have her sit on your face (they love it) while burying your tongue deep in her pussy. I like to call it tongue fucking. You can also do the same from behind. Just stick your tongue in her pussy and shove it in and out with a forceful head thrust. You can grab on to both ass checks and spread them wide open to go deeper. You can also grab on to the ass to push your face into her ass checks while you eat her pussy. A great pleasure amplifier is your thumb. Rub your thumb in a top down motion from her vaginal opening up to her clit, all while you tongue fuck or lick her. How about spreading her ass and licking her asshole – some women will go nuts when you do it and some will cramp up, but how will you (or she) know if she likes it, if you don't try it.

Which brings me to cock sucking – it's a fair assumption that all men like to be sucked off by their woman (unless you are gay and just haven't found the courage to get out of the closet). I therefore hope for the sake of your relationship that your woman gives you head, as otherwise there's a wide gap in your sexual desires that urgently needs to be filled. You shouldn't be ashamed to ask your woman to suck your dick, and you should tell her straight out that you miss it (in case it's not happening or not as frequently as you'd like). However, be ready to reciprocate the gesture by offering to eat her pussy. The unfairness is that we men are much easier to please – meaning that a woman's task of sucking her man and make him come is in general much easier. I'm not saying that expertise and the technique of how to better suck a dick aren't important, because they make a huge difference, and an experienced woman can suck at your cock for an extended time period before she decides it's time for you to shoot your load.

Again, this only confirms that we men are simpler creatures compared to our women. In any case, it doesn't mean that you cannot instruct your woman on how you want her to suck your cock – fast, slow, with a hand stroke, licking your balls, or with a finger up your ass – sometimes you just have to let your woman know what you want. You'll be surprised that many of your wishes may come true, because hopefully she will want to please you the right way. Honest communication can go a long way and positively surprise you.

The next foreplay act is to do it to one another simultaneously – 69 style, of course. Most of you have heard about it and seen it, but many of you don't practice it. This needs to change. I can only assure you that one of the greatest sex pleasures you can experience is to have your woman's ass on your face, while you lick her pussy and she sucks your cock. It intensifies both of your actions; you will lick and eat more pussy, while your woman will suck harder on your cock. It's a win-win situation. Remember, this is what you're aiming for.

Try it also the other way round. Sit on her and stick your cock in her mouth and then move your head down to lick her pussy – just be careful not to shove your cock to deep into her mouth to avoid choking her, although there are women who love to deep-throat a man's dick, which is often accompanied by a choking sensation (some women actually find this pleasurable). If you are physically strong enough, I suggest you try out a different version of the mutual mouth-watering act. Do it standing up. Pick your woman up, hold her upside down and grab her by the waist. Bury your face between her ass checks, while she grabs on to your fuck-stick. Just be sure to know your limits, as you really don't want to accidentally let go of your woman in this situation.

One more thing I'd like to share with you that ensures better oral sex – shave or trim. Of course I am referring to your crotch and this addresses both you and your woman. It's quite an annoying feeling to try and remove a hair that has wandered deep down your throat and persists in remaining there, no matter how hard you try to get it out. This can be easily avoided if you and your woman trim your bushes once in a while or shave them off completely. A shaven pussy is very sexy, and you should encourage your woman to shave or wax it regularly. Some women get turned on by the thought that their pussy hair is all trimmed down or that they pulled a Kojak. Most men get turned on by a clean-shaven or waxed pussy. It intensifies our sexual reaction. We can actually see our entire cock penetrating our woman's pussy, which otherwise is partly covered up by the excess hair.

As I said, this goes both ways. Shave off the excess hair surrounding your cock. Trim it short and shave off the tiny hairs, especially the ones on your balls, if you want your woman to gladly suck at them. Hairy balls are a bummer. You can shave off your hair up to the end of your shaft, which may result in a cock-enlarging effect – yeah, this is true; suddenly your cock appears larger. Some men like it so much that they cannot get enough of admiring their cleanly shaven cock in the mirror, especially when it's all hard and stiff. Your woman will be amazed to see it all cleaned up and it will positively affect her attitude toward sucking you off. Many women and men get excited knowing that their private parts are shaven and they walk around with a horny feeling all day long waiting to come home and fuck their partner. One more warning – if you are a first timer shaving your cock, don't be alarmed if you have an itching sensation the next day. Your hair grows and this causes the itching feeling, but after a few times it passes and it's worth the price, especially when you and your woman don't have to deal any more with "hairy" situations.

THE TRUTH ABOUT PORN

Porn…man's second best friend – Willy is still number one. As much as porn is essential to satisfy our daily sex ration, it is also controversial and many men fall victim to the hyped up world of porn. Porn is great and we all love it. Ever since we were young, and at the tender age of trying to figure out what to do with our dick, we were obsessed with getting hold of our father's or brother's porn magazine or video collection to satisfy our growing urge. We didn't even know why we were so desperately drawn to it, but no matter where it was hidden or locked away, our urge was strong and eventually we found ways to get our hands on it. Where there's a Will(y) there's a way. Our kids of course will have less problem (if at all) to get access to porn, for better or for worse, but here's a reality check – for a man, it's part of growing up, and the best way to cope with porn is to see it for what it really is. In today's world of broadband internet, porn has become a commodity. It is so ubiquitous and easy to come by, whether you are ready to pay for it on specialty websites, view it for free on sites like You Porn, or download gigabytes of it for free (illegally, I must add).

It's a tool to release our pressure and satisfy our daily need for ejaculation, nothing else. We men are such simple creatures; all it takes is for us to see a pair of naked tits, a round ass or a pussy, and our horny hormones kick in. It's a visual trigger that enables us to go from 0-60 in a matter of seconds. The downside is that many men today rely on porn to get into gear, instead of using their imagination to get their juices flowing. Is it too much to ask of you to try and occasionally jerk off to the memories of a classy broad that you fucked in the past or to fantasize about the chick with the perfect ass that you saw for a brief moment passing you on the street? This exercise guarantees that you are not entirely reliant on artificially generated visuals to get your daily fix. Be advised that too much porn can get you down and cause a state of depression – at some point an ass is an ass and a blow job is just another blow job, and then you find yourself (what I like to call) porn-zapping; i.e., skipping through your large porn collection or going online and browsing for hours to find that one porn scene that still turns you on just enough so you can finally come. It's similar to an addiction where you have to up the dosage and try out other drugs to reach your high.

Other men get addicted to the semi-real internet variant. Live video calls/chats. Oh my, what a trap. Although it's the safe form of meeting strange women online, it can quickly evolve into a costly habit which is hard to break (many men are addicted). The overwhelming choice of women who are ready to present themselves naked, and for a few dollars per minute perform sexual acts without inhibition for the millions of men around the world, is growing every day. For men it represents a way to fulfill many of their fantasies, like engaging women of all races and asking them to do the things they do not dare to ask of their women. I say that as long as you are capable of trying it out without falling into the money trap, then go for it. However, as with every emerging industry where there's a lot of money to be made, the innocence or realness of things vanish, and online video channels are being hosted by a growing number of semi-professionals and professionals who do this for a living.

A side note: You should be aware that many of the girls that sell their bodies on online video sites are exploited by online pimps that force these women to perform for extended periods of time at a fraction of the already very low per minute rate that you are willing to pay. So honestly, given these circumstances, how good or real do you think these performances are going to be? If you get hooked, the reality factor diminishes and it becomes nothing less than a highly expensive porn service. My advice to all the men is to save their money and opt for one of the many free alternatives. Look at it this way – the few minutes it takes you to jerk off can add up to an expensive monthly bill. This money is better spent on taking your woman out to a nice dinner and fucking her afterwards. In my book a real pussy (the one of my woman) always beats the virtual pussy of a stranger.

This brings me to the next point. The entire porn industry is a big hoax! Strangely enough, there are just too many men that don't realize this and still think that what they see or are made to believe is actually real. Bull crap!

Big lie #1 – All men have huge cocks.

This is what the industry would like you to think, or why do you think porn flicks are plastered with cocks the size of oversized dildos. The vast majority of men have average size cocks and the chances are high that you do too – which is perfectly fine and more than sufficient to properly satisfy your woman.

Other industries use the same tactics. Just look at the advertising and fashion industry, which is trying to make us believe that all people are beautiful, thin and successful. For this reason they use only people with superlative attributes – very beautiful, very athletic, very thin, very successful, etc.

The porn industry uses many superlatives – huge cocks (the larger the better), big round asses or very small and perfectly trim asses, big tits, thin women, men on steroids, etc. Most of the porn actors are artificially enhanced human beings, and if you saw them in the real world, you would ask yourself why you have been jerking off to these faces for so many years. There is nothing wrong with doing that, just as long as you understand that it has nothing to do with reality. No common woman accepts the offer of a strange man on the street (while she is being filmed) to follow him to a hotel room and then within minutes start sucking his cock, which results in an ass bang. C'mon, be realistic. How many friends do you know that have been so fortunate as to be fucked by two, three, or more women at once? Although it's a great fantasy, it rarely happens. Two girls, well yeah, this occasionally happens, but the more women you pile on top of this fantasy the more unlikely it gets.

So please...don't go trying to grow your cock as promised to you by some crappy online banner advertisement or seek out surgical solutions to add a few inches to your cock size. You are well advised to learn how to fuck your woman the right way, rather than relying solely on your cock size to guarantee her satisfaction.

Big lie #2 – All women love big cocks.

Yeah sure. It's just another myth the porn industry would like us to believe, but if you are observant, you will notice that when some John tries to stick his overly huge cock in a porn actor's pussy or ass, she will often cramp up or push him back (have you noticed that some actors have hurtful facial expressions?). Many of the women that ride or suck those monster cocks are nothing but trained professionals; it takes a lot of training to deep throat one of those monsters without throwing up. Imagine how many times these women were fucked in the ass before they were ready to take it in without flinching once. It still doesn't mean that they are not hurting when an overly huge cock is knocking at their uterus or ripping their asshole apart, but most of these professional ladies are able to suppress their hurtful expressions. I'm not denying that some women like huge cocks, just like many men like huge tits or big asses, but hey, it's not the general rule. In general we people are drawn to larger, better and bigger things in life and so women can be visually attracted to large cocks, but once they experience them, most of them will still prefer to be fucked by an average sized cock that knows what it's doing.

So next time you want to pull out your cock, don't be intimidated by the "wrong" picture the porn industry is projecting. Your cock will do the job, be sure of it.

Big lie #3 – Women always want to fuck spontaneously.

In fact, most women are very different to the women that fuck for money in porn movies. Don't expect your women to be like the women who suck and fuck every person in a matter of minutes. In a porn flick, the average time before a woman gives head or the man finds his face between a woman's legs is 90 seconds. Hello!…in the real world just taking off your clothes takes longer than that, never mind getting into heavy action. Most of the women you see in those productions are deliberately the mental projections of women we men would like to fuck

– equipped with large tits, firm asses and shaved pussies, and preferably in great shape whether they are young or MILFs (Mothers I'd like to fuck), and on top of that they are uninhibited, kinky and always horny. Now look at your woman; many of these attributes will not apply; but there is one big difference: your woman is the real thing.

Embrace it. There is something very sexy and attractive about fucking a real woman, and once you understand it, you will be able to enjoy a porn flick for what it is, an enjoyable few minutes that helps you spurt your load. On another note, I would like to add here that even the porn industry is not immune to ever-changing trends. What men might have considered yesterday to be a sexy, erotic and cock-stiffening image of a woman is today less appealing. For example, the female porn stars of today are not the slim and trim women of the eighties and nineties, but rather much more voluptuous, with huge racks and big asses. Nowadays big is very sexy, and it seems that men are realizing that more is really more, and that we prefer our women with a few more pounds in the right places. Let your woman in on this secret and tell her that her ass is just the way you want it and that fucking a bigger ass is more exciting to you than humping a small one that has less to grab.

As long as you understand this, your will still be turned on by your woman, even if she has at some point lost some of the attributes you wish she still had. If your woman never possessed these attributes from the start, maybe now you will be less disappointed, knowing that you were drawn to an imaginary personification of female beauty. Take a good look at yourself; most likely you don't get a perfect score yourself, but nonetheless you would want your woman to love (oops I used the L word) you for what you are. This goes both ways of course.

Big lie #4 – A good fuck is a long lasting fuck.

I really hope you are not misled by the illusion that men were built to fuck their women for hours and hours. In general, the actual fuck lasts for a few minutes only. It's comparable to a chef that prepares a great dish for a few hours only to see it devoured in a matter of minutes. Still, this doesn't diminish the culinary satisfaction in any way. A good meal always remains a good meal and is often remembered for days, if not years, to come. The same principle applies to a good fuck. Most men are oblivious to the fact that porn studs are chosen not only for their large cock but also for their ability to last as long as possible. Many men trying out as porn actors don't make the cut or are required to attain the required endurance by training certain muscles (the muscle between the ass and crotch) or applying mind control techniques to avoid premature ejaculation.

Are you even aware that, as with every other type of production, a porn flick isn't shot in one take and that male porn actors can pause in between takes to calm down their urge or shoot of their load? So why don't you do the same? Whenever you feel that you are reaching the point of no return and you want to prolong the fuck, then call for a time out. Let your woman know that you don't want to come yet as you are enjoying it too much, and believe me, she will understand. However, to take five doesn't imply that you lie at her side and do nothing. You have to maintain the sexual tension or your woman will lose her itch. Kiss her, eat her pussy, or suck her nipples; anything goes that will keep her in the zone, and once you have recuperated, hop back in the saddle and take her for another ride.

There are, of course, measures you can take to extend your stamina. Pharmaceuticals, drugs and alcohol will have the desired effect on your stamina and they will also increase sensation levels. I, for example, can go on alcohol for hours, but be aware that you don't revert to these forms of artificial sex boosters to get your cock up (and stay up) to satisfy your woman. I will not argue that it can be lots of fun to use these uppers from time to time, but be very careful about using them frequently, as they will lose the desired effect if consumed too often. It can down spiral out of control and you may find yourself continuously upping the dosage or reverting to stronger drugs and stimuli to get a kick, and then, my man, you have a very big problem on your hands. I know for a fact that many men are unable to fuck their woman without having to first pop some pills or sniff some rows of blow to get into the mood. You really don't want to find yourself in this category and if you already are, then get some help. Sex is still best in its natural form, and the chemical cocktail released in your brain during an orgasm is still the best high you can get.

I would also like to point out that there is nothing wrong with a quicky from time to time. However, this implies that you already know your woman very well and know how to make her reach her peak in a few minutes. If you rip off her clothes, stick your dick into her pussy and then come after a few strokes without giving her an orgasm, then you just lost the game. Always go for the Win-Win situation, remember? Therefore make sure your woman is horny enough to short cut her long ascent to her peak before you decide to hump her, or next time she might have reservations and deny you the pleasure of a quicky.

Having said all that…from time to time you will still find yourself in the position where you came too soon or too fast and your woman didn't reach an orgasm. Don't be frustrated if this happens; it is normal and being a man means that you will have to cope with this type of situation for as long as you can get it up. You might have been too excited going into the fuck, which is why you came faster than usual, or maybe you haven't fucked for a long period of time, or you didn't jerk off the night before. As long as it is the exception, you are safe, but let your woman know why you came that quickly. Telling her the reason will show her that you are considerate of her needs, and she will happily accept and dismiss you premature ejaculation.

Big lie #5 – One cock, lots of pussies; one pussy, many cocks.

Crap! Every second porn scene shows a man fucking more than one woman or several men fucking one woman. This is so far from reality. Sure, men have fantasies of fucking several women at once, and when you look at porn flicks you could actually believe that every man is capable of doing it. Well, most of us are not. There are also women who fantasize of having two or more cocks pleasing them at once, but taking into account that women also seek an emotional connection in bed, then fucking with a bunch of strange men is rather unlikely or the exception to the rule. Now, as long as we confine these types of situations to a movie, we men can handle it.

However, the second we transgress these scenarios into reality, we quickly out these women as sluts. It's in our nature to stamp women with an excessive sex drive and the lust for more than one cock as sluts. Our belief tells us that only a slut or prostitute would do this. As long as the slut is not our woman, then all is fine, but no man will want to even remotely think that his woman is sucking another man's dick, let alone, is being fucked by another man or several for that matter – we men cannot even stand the thought of our woman kissing another man. It's in human nature (especially in the male gene pool) to protect what is ours, and it doesn't get more personal than protecting our piece of pussy. So next time you watch a porn scene, with a multitude of bodies engaged in sucking and fucking each other, keep in mind that it's very much against your underlying relationship values.

Fantasizing about it and jerking off to it are very different from exploring such an opportunity, which in real life rarely happens, and when it does it is often with the help of illegal trickery (getting the woman drugged or drunk), paying hookers, or going to swinger clubs. Here is another thought…you better be damn secure in your relationship and in full control of your emotions, if you decide to take your woman to a swinger club or swinger party. What at first glance might be a new and exciting way to bring fun into your sex life can quickly turn very ugly when feelings of jealousy and betrayal rise to the surface. Be prepared to have the images of your woman riding a strange cock or getting ass banged by two strangers deeply burned into your mind forever. Furthermore, what might have been a fun day for you might easily have been a nightmare experience for your woman, and this type of situation can quickly turn nasty, reaching levels of anger and distrust that down the road can lead to a nasty breakup.

Is there any other value that porn provides? Yes indeed. It's highly educational. You might say that is contradictory to what I argue, and you are right to some extent, but I very much believe that good porn can broaden the sexual horizon of men and can help to educate men in the art of fucking. Good porn flicks are like video tutorials if you omit all the exaggerated superlatives (big dicks, huge tits, etc.) and cheesy plots. I am proud to say that I picked up some of my best moves watching porn and trying them out the next time the opportunity presented itself. Porn can give you some good ideas on how to fuck your woman, and because of its uninhibited nature, it gives a shit about the social rules of engagement. You should make it your goal to consume a broad range of porn, including one-on-one scenes, anal, lesbian, orgy, inter-racial and so forth. This will expose you to a lot of new kinky ideas and keep you from staying within your pornographic comfort zone. Often porn watching is confined to a certain sexual preference, fetish or ethnic group, and you should find ways to dismiss your prejudicial mind set, as you may never know if seeing a hot lesbian or hard core anal scene could give you the edge when you fuck your woman the next time.

The challenge for you is to see porn for what it really is. Don't take any of the female actress's moaning, crying and verbal outcries of joy and amazement for real. Most of what you see rarely indicates a woman's approval of how she is being fucked or the level of satisfaction she is experiencing. This, my fellow men, you will have to find out on your own the next time you fuck your woman, by using a new technique, trying out a novel fuck position, or seeking out a daring location. Go for it!

ENJOY THE TOY

Ever used some frivolous toys to please your woman? You definitely should try it out if you haven't. Nowadays there are so many toys to choose from, and in today's internet era it is so easy to mail order if you want to avoid embarrassing excursions to the neighborhood sex shop. Please…there is no reason to be ashamed of being seen at a sex shop; it proves that you are confident in your sexuality and that you are proactively seeking to spice up your sex life, and that's a good thing. The stuff you can find there certainly benefits women and men alike – so why are many men reluctant to make use of toys?

Here are some of the main reasons: First of all, there's intimidation. A lot of men are intimidated by the sizes of some of the toys (dildos and vibrators, of course) and are terrified at the thought that once they try them out on their women, it might put them at a disadvantage, should their women develop an affection for size. By now you should have understood that a good fuck is not entirely measured by the size of a dick and certainly not by an artificial cock-like object. Instead of being petrified by the thought of needing to compete with a toy ('cause that's all it is) you should plan it into your sex routine. Exude confidence when you pull it out to surprise your woman, and by the way, there is no telling if your woman isn't already using a super-sized dildo or vibrator without your knowledge. One thing you should always keep in mind is that nothing beats the real thing, and furthermore, a toy is only as good as its handler.

Then there's shame. The question must be: why are men so uncomfortable with revealing their sexual fantasies, and why do they choose to keep them bottled up? Many men are even ashamed to confess that they have dirty thoughts about using toys on their woman. There is no reason why you should be. Set your so-called "what you were taught to be appropriate sex" values aside, and toss those shameful feelings overboard. Chances are you grew up in a suppressed sexual environment, and it's about time you tore yourself loose from those misinformed attitudes. It is a lot of fun to browse the net for special toys or to wander through the aisles of a sex shop to find the one contraption that could bring joy to your woman. Have it gift wrapped and see her wondrous face as she unwraps the package to reveal an unexpected surprise. Tell her confidently that you would like to try it out on her and that you want to play with her using the toy or toys – and be ready for a positive reaction. She might not jump you right away – women still need to be in the mood, you know – but be assured that when the time comes, she will happily remind you to pull out the tools of joy.

Start out with the basics like a dildo or vibrator before you branch out to the more exotic toys – you do not want to frighten your woman from the get go; your objective is to get her acquainted with another fun and playful way to improve and enjoy fucking and sex in general. If your woman is the conservative one in your relationship, and if it is she who is ashamed or disgusted at the thought of you sticking toys in her sex holes, then by all means, you should talk to her about it and ask her to try it out. It's up to you to take the lead on this subject and show her the ways of pleasure she may not be aware of. How can one tell if a dish is delicious without tasting it? From my experience, most women don't know what they like in sex until they eventually experience it, and even the most conservative and retained woman will succumb to the proposal of a potentially good fuck with the lure of a potential multiple orgasms.

The third reason is homophobia. C'mon...I know that some of you out there actually believe that holding a dildo in your hand is like holding another man's cock. There is not much I can say on this subject, apart from that you are a complete idiot. Get over it.

Now that we've elaborated on some of the issues that might prevent you from using sex toys, here's a short overview of some of the toys you should try out with your woman. There is such a rich variety out there, and new ones are being invented as we speak, but I would like to draw your attention to the ones that, from my experience, work best. As a general rule, please make sure to have a lubricant at hand; a silicon based gel or oil is best. Some of the toys are better lubed up before usage to allow for easy penetration and a smooth gliding feeling. If there is none at hand, make sure to use enough spit or wait for your woman's pussy to be wet enough and use her juices as lube (BTW the same is relevant of your dick; longer fuck sessions require a lube or enough spit to keep the pussy moist).

The dildo – it's the most popular toy for sexual pleasure, but not to be confused with its close cousin, the vibrator. The dildo comes in many shapes, sizes and materials – from metal to plastic to rubber, from small to large, and from straight as a candle to curved as a hook. Some of them look like bad imitations of our cocks, whereas others are slick and often look like design objects. They can be double-headed or long and flexible to enable double penetration. The other option of course is to use two dildos, a larger one for the pussy and smaller one for the anus (some like it vice versa). The main difference compared to a vibrator is that it's not motorized and it doesn't vibrate, twist, turn or pump. It's a great toy for teasing your woman by running it across her pussy lips and stimulating her clit. Alternate between pussy and asshole, and let your woman suck on it from time to time. Think of the dildo as an extension of your fingers, and be playful.

Once you start dildo fucking your woman, be gentle at first, and then change the tempo and the force of your thrusts to extend the pleasure level. Alternate also between a twisting and a straight thrust motion, and let her try to squeeze out the toy with her vaginal or rectal muscles.

Of course, all of the toys can be used in foreplay or while fucking your woman. There are two types of double penetration that you can try out (in case you didn't know). Simply stick your dick in your preferred hole and use the dildo to penetrate the other one, or stick your dick in the same hole as the dildo (in this case you better make sure your woman is wide open to avoid hurting her). Most of the women that haven't been fortunate enough to experience a double penetration will cry out in joy when both of their holes are stuffed simultaneously, and I urge you to be the first man that does this toher.The memory of the first double penetration stays presentin your woman's mind (just like the first anal fuck) and it brings you both closer (needless to say, you must make sure it's a positive and memorable experience).

The vibrator – many women refer to it as their best friend, especially single women, but they all would happily trade it in for a real cock that knows how to fuck them right (straight women, of course). Today vibrators look like high-tech toys. They are like Swiss army knives, which offer a myriad of tools in one compact shape, and they have evolved from the simple vibrating dildo-type into winding, turning, pumping and rotating contraptions. They promise to make women experience better orgasms. Some of the vibrators, at least to me, look like objects from outer space that might easily have been created by some alien race to satisfy the sexual needs of their female equivalents. Some of them twist in different directions simultaneously and use different speeds for each of the oscillating parts, which, by the way, may also use different textures, such as knobs in various sizes and softness. Then there are certain models, often referred to as rabbit vibrators, that come with a second extension to stimulate the clit or with a third extension for simultaneous anal penetration. To me, it appears that women are made to believe that vibrators are the ultimate orgasm generators and that with a few hundred bucks and a stash of alkaline batteries, all the wishes for the ultimate orgasm can be realized.

True, these devices work really well, as they have been designed by people who have studied and been instructed in women's physiology. Imagine how many women must have tested these devices to approve their functionality. So rather than being threatened by these devices, you should be happy that they exist, and you should be happy if your woman uses them to satisfy her abundant sex drive. Be considerate and ask her what she especially likes about these devices, and what they do to her to make her come. You can learn from this, and the next time you do your handiwork or eat her pussy, you can try to imitate or apply some of the techniques that work wonders on specific parts of her sexual organs, specifically the clit and G-spot area. Maybe you'll find out that she enjoys filling both of her holes at the same time, but that she was too ashamed to ask you or didn't know how you could accomplish that. Women that masturbate know their bodies better than women that don't. They can playfully try out things without committing to them and figure out if they enjoy certain techniques that they may not have experienced yet with their partners. Imagine that one day your woman simply grabs your cock and sticks it up her ass. Yes, this really happens and it can only stem from a previous pleasurable experience she has had; hopefully it was only a vibrator that expanded her sexual horizon. As with dildos, be confident enough to include vibrators in your sex routine. Use them during foreplay and while you are fucking your woman to achieve extended levels of pleasure.

Butt plugs – now here's a naughty device. As simple as it is, its applicative use is very naughty and very sexy. Of course butt plugs can be used either to get your woman acquainted with the experience of anal pleasures or to step up the anal fucking experience. Again, they come in various shapes and sizes, and they can be made of various materials like rubber, silicone, plastic and metal. Some women that fancy anal (and there are a lot of them out there) can walk around for many hours with a butt plug stuck up their ass. Of course they love the idea that no one around them knows that underneath their clothes they are sexy sluts. Some women really get a kick out of being a slut in bed and to those men I say, congrats, make sure you give your woman the space she needs to explore and play out her sexual fantasies with you. First timers to butt plugs should use smaller plugs in the beginning and lube them to reduce any hurting sensation when sticking them in their ass. You should insert the plug slowly and not be discouraged if it doesn't go in all the way. You should gently expand your woman's asshole until she is relaxed enough to take in the plug at its thickest point. Once she overcomes the thickest point, she will experience a relaxing sensation when the plug slides in all the way.

The butt plug is of course a great tool to prepare your woman for anal fucking, so chances are that if your woman grants you the pleasure of butt plugging her ass, than she may be ready for the next step, which is hard core anal. Still, a butt plug up your woman's ass doesn't necessarily mean that she wants you to ass fuck her. It can be a work in progress and maybe after a few more times she will be ready for your dick (more on anal in the following chapter). In the meantime you should enjoy the moment and her readiness to expand her sexual boundaries. Rest assured that she will experience a great orgasm if you choose to fuck her pussy with a butt plug stuck up her ass.

Love beads – this is a fun toy, which is basically a string of balls available in various sizes and materials. These balls are carefully inserted into a woman's anus, one after the other, for a twofold pleasure, once when you push them in, and then again when you pull at the string to get them out. As with any anal toy, it is always good to first finger and relax the asshole before moving on to the toy. You should use a lube if you are new to this sort of fun. Of course you can insert the beads into the pussy as well, but most likely you will need to use larger beads to achieve the desired pleasurable sensation.

Cock rings – some men are just too homophobic to even think of using a cock ring, but I can assure you that in can very much increase the pleasure for you and your woman. The right size of cock ring will accurately limit the blood flow to your cock, which results in longer fuck sessions by extending the time before you spurt off. This of course gives you the ability to fuck your woman harder and longer and gives you the edge to make her come. Some of the ring models are designed to stimulate your woman's clit. These models are equipped with a nub extension on the ring to come in contact with your woman's clit with every stroke of your cock. This of course will make your woman come faster.

So keep an open mind and try wearing a cock ring. Women can find it very sexy to see their man's cock decorated with a cock ring, since it is one of the few toys design-ed especially for men and it testifies to your male confidence and your readiness to better satisfy your woman. Wearing a cock ring improves and enhances the real thing and is not just another cock-like substitute.

The love swing – also known as the sex swing, is definitely one of the ultimate sex toys and is an excellent tool to improve your sex life. It enables you to experience sexual positions with ease that might otherwise be difficult to achieve. A love swing defies gravity and gives you control to fuck your woman in ways she has never been fucked before. It gives you better control to explore your woman's body and reach the deepest and most sensitive areas in your woman's vagina. The love swing is a harness, especially designed to induce sexual pleasures, and its use goes way back in history. Basically, your woman is securely suspended in mid air and can succumb to every sexual move lined up for her. Her buttocks are comfortably positioned at the height of your dick, which gives you excellent control during the fuck. You can easily grab on to her ass and waist and pull her towards you with every stroke to increase the force of your thrusts. You can do your woman from the front, back, from above and from beneath. Your woman places her legs in the attached loops or uses them as stirrups to actively control her movements. She can also just lean back and let you do all the work, while she enjoys a relaxing position with her legs spread wide open. It's the ultimate flexible contraption, giving you a myriad of ways to let your fantasies run wild and enjoy sex. The great thing about the love swing is that you can take turns and alternate between being the one who gives pleasure to your woman and being the one that gets pampered. Having your cock sucked while suspended in midair is a joyful experience, as is having your woman mount you while you are in a very comfortable position. The best part, however, is that you are experiencing together a lot of new ways to please each other and finding out more about your partner. It's comparable to a sex dance. One last important piece of advice: make sure you chose a good quality love swing that doesn't collapse in the middle of a heated fuck session.

Handcuffs, ropes and blindfolds – although they don't fall into the classic toy category, they definitely belong in the group of basic sex tools. Handcuffs are not usually readily on hand, but belts or scarves can be a substitute for ropes, and any long piece of cloth can be used to create a blindfold. If you haven't figured it out by now, then let me tell you that the actual toy is the tied-up person (your woman). There is something very exciting about being tied up to the bed or a chair without the ability to control the situation. It's that helplessness that forces us to accept whatever sexual fantasy our partner wants to fulfill. Women, even strong women, occasionally like to be submissive and hand over full control to their partners. It is here and now that you can take charge and try out the things you have never dared to do. When your woman is blindfolded and tied up, there is not much she can do to discourage you. There is no disapproving look or rejecting body language to stop your advancement. You should seize the moment to explore your woman's body and satisfy your needs. Once your woman has decided to hand over the reins to you, she will expect you to know what you want. Most importantly, you have to take your time to tease and play with your woman for as long as possible. It's a mind game…your woman will try to figure out what it is you want to do to her, and the uncertainty, together with the inability to object, will trigger her excitement. You have to continuously tease her – touch her, then lick different parts of her body, then finger her, and then stick your cock in her mouth. At any time you should be unpredictable, never letting her know what to expect next. You could even decide to shave her pussy, or pour honey or chocolate syrup over her body and pussy lips and indulge in a long and tasty pussy eating session. Anything goes and the more creative you are, the better, and the more your woman is going to love it. You can alternate between fucking her and playing with her. Always keep her hanging on the edge of an orgasm and extend the pleasurable feeling without making her come. The longer you can prolong the time before she experiences her first orgasm, the more intense it will be, and once she comes, you should aim for a multiple orgasm.

What you are doing in this situation is much more than pleasing your woman; you are strengthening the feeling of trust between you and your woman, and the more she enjoys what you are doing to her, the more she is going to open up to you and let you do to her whatever you desire. Still, you should stay alert at all times and watch out for signals of uneasiness or discomfort. Whatever you do to your woman while she is under your control, remember to do it gradually and respectfully and chances are she will love every moment of it. The next step is to switch roles and let your woman decide what she would like to do to you. Once again, you might be very surprised to learn that she is totally enjoying it, more than you thought she would. Contrary to what you might believe, giving up control and handing it over to your woman affirms to her that you are very self-assured about your manhood and that you can set your macho demeanor aside to enjoy the ride. In her eyes that makes you a sexy man.

BACKDOOR TO HEAVEN

What is it about anal fucking that we men like so much? Have we ever asked ourselves if we are gay on some deeper level? What makes us so horny when we think of sticking our dick in a woman's asshole? Some may argue that it's the tightness of the asshole that increases our sexual pleasure and makes us want it so bad. Surely there is truth in that, but there's much more to it. I say it's the idea of having nasty sex and being the man that fucks your woman in ways she was never fucked before or knowing that you are the only one doing her in the ass . If you are an ass fetishist, then you will agree that there is nothing more beautiful and sexy than a woman's ass facing you and teasing you to do all kinds of nasty things with it. Women can easily increase our desire by spreading their cheeks apart and showing us just how much they want and trust us to fuck them.

Doing your woman's ass has a lot to do with trust. Know that your woman is really into you if she is willing to take your dick up her ass and that she trusts you a lot. She knows you are going to try and keep the hurt to a minimum (anal sex is especially hurtful to the novice). She will expect you to know that you need to be gentle, before you can get rough. We men often need to be very persuasive to get our women to open the backdoor and let us in. Don't take it for granted; it is a gift you have to earn and it is handed out for extremely good behavior. The art is to do it right the first time as it can be very traumatic to women, and if you literally fuck it up, you will have a hard time convincing your woman that anal can be really fun (for her). The truth is that it really can be, and there are enough women that will testify that they love to be fucked in the ass. These women were lucky to have an experienced man, one who knew his way around a woman's ass, to introduce them to the world of anal sex. There is no reason why you cannot be one of these men.

Anal sex needs a slow build up; you cannot just stick your dick in the anus and hope for the best. The anus is a muscle that needs to be gently expanded before it can welcome your cock. Denying it the acquaintance phase will likely result in a shut backdoor manned by a very cautious home owner who will make sure that no unexpected guest tries to pick the lock. You have to be subtle and clever and know how far you can go during the sex session without your woman rejecting your advances. So what should you do? The gentlest approach is to lick your woman's ass while eating her pussy. Switch between pussy and ass, and test the ground. You can tell if she is into it if she doesn't cramp up when your tongue touches her anus. Once this is established you can step up your tongue action by pushing your tongue gently into her asshole. Always make sure she is not cramping up, and while you lick or tongue fuck her asshole you should massage her clit. It is of utmost importance that your woman stays relaxed at all times or her ass muscle will cramp up. Playing with her clit will help her to stay relaxed and keep her ass open and penetrable.

The next step is to massage her anus with one of your fingers, but make sure not to penetrate her. You have to step up your game gradually and slowly. Your woman needs to feel that you are doing everything in your power not to hurt her. She must be convinced that what you are doing is fun, exciting and pleasurable. After you verify that your woman isn't opposed to your anus massage, you can try to insert your pinkie into her asshole, but make sure that your finger is slippery. Use spit or lube before sticking your finger in her ass. Do it slowly, and again make sure your woman doesn't cramp up. Especially when you enter your finger for the first time, you will encounter a slight resistance, but once your finger is inside, the muscle begins to relax. Keep your finger inside her without moving it around too much. You need to give your woman the time to adjust to this new sensation, as she is still not sure if she likes or hates it. After a few moments you can start to finger fuck her slowly. Gently push your finger in and out of her ass until you feel that she is widening up. Again you can spit on her ass to keep her hole wet and slippery. Only then can you switch to a larger finger, either index or middle. At all times, while you are fingering her ass, make sure to lick or massage her pussy. I cannot emphasize it enough; it helps your woman to relax her anus.

You now have two options: either you can increase the radius of your finger action to expand the asshole or you can use one of the many toys to do it. When opting for a toy, make sure it is lubed up before you stick it in her ass. This is now the test you have been waiting for. If she accepts the toy and enjoys it, then she is ready for your cock. At some point, remove the toy and replace it with your cock, but make sure you use a lot of spit or lube on your dick. Stick your cock slowly into your woman's ass, but don't make the mistake of pushing it in all the way, as it could hurt your woman. Once your cock is inside her, you should start to fuck her slowly and only up the tempo after several long and deep strokes. No matter what you do, don't take out your cock at this stage or you will not get it back in again. Whether you are fucking her in the ass from behind or while she is lying on her back, don't forget to play with her pussy (at least in the beginning until she is relaxed enough and starts enjoying the ass fuck).

Your objective is to make sure your woman doesn't cramp up with your dick up her ass, as it will hurt you as well if her ass muscle squeezes off the blood supply to your dick. Be creative and use one of the toys to fuck her pussy while you fuck her ass. Giving your woman a double penetration could result in a very strong and intense orgasm. If she comes, keep your cock in her ass, even if she is squeezing off your cock, even if it hurts a bit. Having your dick inside her while she comes will only intensify her orgasm and this is what you want.

Some women will squirt when you ass fuck them, as it stimulates their G-spot. Let's hope for you that your woman is a squirter, since it will be for her the best outcome she could wish for. Once she starts squirting, continue to slide your fingers in and out of her pussy so she might experience a serial squirt. I can assure you that if you get her to squirt several times in a row, she will look at you with different eyes from that moment on.

An important tip I need to give you is that you never know when your woman is going to be ready for anal. Even if she already went through an ass fuck with you, it still doesn't mean that every time you have sex, you can fuck her in the ass. Therefore, take advantage of those rare moments when all the stars are aligned to grant you your wish (some women do it only to satisfy their partner). Some of you will be luckier, as there are many women who really like anal and will want you to fuck them in the ass regularly. It's up to you to find out which type of women you are fucking.

If your woman likes anal (if she does, there will be no doubt about it) then you could go so far as to stick your cock up your woman's ass without any warning, but you have to make sure that she is very horny when you try a sneak attack (even if she likes being fucked in the ass). The success rate of a sneak attack can turn out to be lower than the methodological approach, so take this into consideration.

DRESS UP, SEX UP

Okay, here's an issue close to my heart: dressing up and sexing up – the first one being sexy clothing and the second one being what I like to call slut wear. The line between sexy and slutty is blurry, and depending on your woman, she can get probably away with both. I am not going to argue about taste, and everyone has the freedom to choose what they want to wear, but I am insisting that we men have the right to ask our women to dress for the occasion. Some women ignore the stimulating effect it has on us men to see our woman dressed up in sexy garments. If you are the victim of your women's ignorance in tending to your visual senses, then it is your job to change it by making her aware of it.

Women that dress sexy are more in tune with their sexuality and unconsciously more open to sexual advances, It is a known fact that certain clothing influences the way we feel, whether we are men or women. It heightens our sense of sexual excitement if we look in the mirror and like what we see. Obviously, we men let our imagination run wild when we see women dressed in clothing that emphasizes their assets. First of all, you could let your woman know that you'd like her to dress sexier because it turns you on. Be encouraging by letting her know that her ass looks great in tight jeans, or that her tits look better in a waisted blouse or tighter t-shirt. When she changes her look to please you, tell her she looks sexy, and always let her know if you like what she is wearing, especially if it turns you on. Undress her with your eyes and say the right words (use a mix of gallant and blunt expressions to express your approval).

Be aware that women are very sensitive about this subject and often use clothes to hide what they believe are their bad features. Often these feelings of inferiority are unsubstantiated. How many women do you know that possess a great body but hide it under baggy clothes? How many women do you know that have beautiful legs but never wear skirts? The list goes on and on. I am sure you have witnessed this behavior with your woman as well. Occasionally we see just how wrong these women are when we are fortunate enough to see them in a bathing suit or bikini, and then we look surprised, scratch our heads, and wonder why they were hiding all that time. Don't let your woman be a woman that holds back on her femininity by wearing unsexy clothing. You want your woman to be one of the women that you like staring at on the street, just long enough so you can check out their ass or rack.

This brings me to the next subject. Are you staring at your woman? I mean are you looking at her with a glance that tells her that you are undressing her with your eyes and that you want to fuck her? Most men lose that stare once they are in a longer relationship, which is very unfortunate. As I said earlier, women like to be stared at; it's a confirmation of their external appearance and they surely want their men to stare at them. So ask yourself why you aren't, and then see if there is anything you can tell your woman to do to get you interested again. Often it doesn't take much to get us men back on track – we're very simple creatures, if you recall. I, for example, wonder why so many women still wear regular panties when it's a known fact that we men are irresistibly turned on by thongs. Is your woman oblivious to the fact that wearing regular panties in tight clothing is sexually unpleasing? We like to pretend our women are naked underneath their pants and skirts, and seeing the lines of their panties is nothing but a big turn off. On the other hand, if we get an unexpected glimpse of the thong she is wearing (when she bends over for example), it sets off an immediate sexual trigger in our brain, which easily causes a hard on. If your woman isn't wearing thongs, then get her to do so, even if it means facilitating the change yourself by going out and buying her a set of sexy thongs.

I still haven't met a woman that doesn't like lingerie. It gives women a sense of sexiness when they wear those small and beautifully decorated pieces of cloth that barely cover their pussy. I recommend that you surprise your woman from time to time with a nice set of lingerie. Any money you invest in this respect is well spent, since you are the main beneficiary. I, for example, like to watch my woman get out of the shower, pick out a thong and then go through her wardrobe to choose what to wear. A woman's ass wearing a thong is pure eye candy and it turns me on every time I see it.

It's a good feeling to fantasize throughout the day about what kind of panties your woman is wearing, and then wait for the moment when you are home to see her take off her clothes to surprise you with exceptionally sexy lingerie. Don't underestimate the importance of sexy underwear, and help your woman to understand that it's important to you.

Let's now move on to slut wear. This is very different from the daily dress code. Slut wear is the visual expression of how we would like to see our woman dress up to fuck. Some woman love to dress up in slut wear, whereas others need a gentle push to be exposed to the limitless varieties of sex-inducing clothing. It's like role play – we men need to know that underneath all those feminine layers is a whore, ready to please us in ways we fantasize about. We have to make our women understand that, for us men, the whore represents a crucial personality we expect to find in our women. Often it is up to us to awake the whore within our woman, as it may be locked away or buried deep under all those layers of socially imposed behavioral patterns. The best place to unleash your woman's "whore" for the first time is in the private surroundings of your home. Women have a problem ascertaining what type of whore we would like them to be, which is of course due to the lack of communication between men and women. Some women act very surprised when they learn that their man wants them to step into the role of a naughty and dirty slut. So men, don't be shy; discuss the subject as if it is a normal and commonly accepted request in a relationship (which it is) that until today hasn't been addressed. Be straightforward and tell your woman what you want her to wear when the time for fucking arrives, or even better, go out and buy the outfits you would like her to wear, then present her with the outfits you have chosen. They will speak for themselves and convey your expectations, facilitating her transition to the whore personality. You will be surprised how many women get sexed up and horny once they wear these sexy outfits. For women it presents the opportunity to step into a role they might have been suppressing for a long time and are eager to let loose (on you).

Again, a huge variety of sexy outfits awaits you, and part of the fun is to find the ones that really turn you on and to imagine them on your woman's body. Still, there are a few outfits that I think work best for most of us men and should be part of your woman's slut wear collection.

Stockings and garter belts – yeah…in the end this is the

all time favorite. If your woman hasn't yet posed for you wearing stockings attached to a garter belt, then you have been missing out big time. What is it that gets us so turned on to see a woman wear those things? Nearly every second or third porn flick we watch has women wearing them, and not without reason. A woman wearing this outfit is dressed up for the occasion, and shows off just enough naked skin to accentuate her pussy and ass. A garter belt and stockings projects the image of a classy whore – a woman that knows how to take care of herself, but still is ready to go all the way and turn into the slutty personality we are hooked on. When you fuck your woman wearing these, the greatest sensation is to alternate between her naked skin and the parts of her body that are covered by the garment. Especially when you take your woman from behind you can see the erotic effect it has. Seeing that ass sandwiched between the stockings and the garter belt is a major turn-on.

Use this as a basic outfit and combine it with various tops like brassieres, corsets, bustiers or a silk night gown to increase the sexually arousing effect. In general, try to enjoy the outfit your woman is wearing and keep your inner animal locked up for as long as possible. Ask your woman to walk around and present to you what she is wearing. Tell her to turn around and show you her ass and have per pose in naughty positions. Whatever you do, don't hide the fact that it's turning you on. Share with her how sexy and beautiful she is looking, and don't be afraid to be blunt about it. You can take out your cock to show her how hard you are, and that you are really enjoying what she is wearing. A tip – instruct your woman to put her thong on top of the garter belt, this way you don't have to unclip the stockings to remove the panties when you are ready to fuck her.

Body/cat suits – one of my favorites. It's a full body outfit that accentuates all your woman's assets through a tightly fitting suit from top to bottom. It comes in net, silk, latex or nylon stretch, and some provide an opening in the crotch area, which is very sexy. An irresistible view is when your woman is wearing a full body latex suit and she bends over to show you her ass. The latex sits tightly on her ass like a second skin and emphasizes the roundness of her cheeks. Now imagine that in this very moment she opens the zipper between her legs to reveal her swollen pussy. All you will be able to focus on is this small area between her ass cheeks, and it will take every bit of your self control not to jump her and stick your cock in her pussy. Try it out!

Hot pants – these are tight and very short pants that highlight the roundness of your woman's ass and her crotch area. Mostly they are available in a stretch fabric or latex and offer a zipper reaching from her ass all the way up between her legs to her crotch. Other models are designed with a cut out area to provide full access to your woman's pussy and ass.

Boots and stilettos – everything your woman wears looks sluttier and sexier when she wears high heels, either as stilettos or thigh-length-high boots. The womanly psyche changes in high heels; her legs appear longer and her walk is sexier. Have you had your woman walk around for you naked in high heels? You will see her ass bouncing in ways you have never known before, and often these extra inches of height are an advantage when you are fucking your woman in a standing position, or if she is riding your cock while you're lying on a bench or sitting on a chair. For reasons of comfort, many women avoid wearing high heels, but at least they should have a pair in their wardrobe to go with their slut wear.

Gloves – of course I am referring to long gloves; some women may know them as prom gloves. They fall into the category of slutty accessories and should be part of your woman's wardrobe. They are best in leather or latex and in black (although some prefer them in red), and what makes them so sexy is their ability to make our women appear slimmer and sexier, especially if they are worn as part of a latex outfit or together with high boots. Have you ever been jerked of by your woman wearing gloves? Exactly…if you haven't, then once again you do not know what you're missing. The sensation of leather or latex stroking your cock is very arousing, and who knows? Your woman might get a kick out of the leather/latex wear and it might open a completely new sexual direction for you. Maybe next time she will use a whip or tie you up, and maybe you're the type of man that likes to be dominated after all.

I would also like to point out that dressing sexy is not limited to women only. We men have many options to package ourselves in a more presentable and fuck-invitingmanner. It starts with the briefs or underwear we choose to wear. Try to alternate between the regular boxer short and a tight-fitting version that accentuates your ass and package. Women can get aroused if they see your hard-on squeezed into tight briefs. Also there are various latex pants and body outfits we men can wear. You will be amazed what effect they have on women. Women also get aroused by certain outfits, and having your cock stick out of a tight latex outfit might get your woman all sexed up and ready to stroke or suck it.

As I said earlier, there are many more options out there that you can try out, and I urge you to check out the thousands of websites that sell these outfits and order one or two for starters, or maybe you just want to visit the nearest sex shop to check them out in person.

SEXCUSES

"I have a headache." This is possibly the most in-use excuse by women to let us know that fucking her is out of the question. How about: "I'm too tired" or "I have to get up early tomorrow" or "I had a tough day" or "I'm in the middle of something" or "What about the kids?" I am sure we have all heard and used some of these sex stoppers in the course of our relationship.

We all have excuses for not doing this and that. Our life is filled with lost opportunities that we try to justify with excuses, and when it comes to sex, it's no different. Regardless of who uses more sexcuses – men or women – in the end, too many sexcuses can damage your sex life.

That said, if I had to determine the female/male ratio for using sexcuses in a relationship to discourage sexual encounters, it would have to be 80:20 in favor of women, which means women use four times more sexcuses than men. Lately, however, this ratio seems to be changing and it appears that more and more men are reverting to lame sexcuses to avoid fucking their women. And this is a disturbing fact. There is something fundamentally wrong with men that use a lot of sexcuses to avoid fucking their woman. As stated previously, fucking is deeply entrenched in the male DNA, and seeking ways to avoid this ultimate form of pleasure is something that needs to be examined. Sex is a mind game. Both men and women (women far more) are influenced by their state of mind when it comes to responding to the chemical reaction that causes the urge to fuck. If you men are able to recognize the causes of these sexual short circuits, you might be able to avoid your sex switch from malfunctioning. There are few plausible reasons for not wanting to do it, but there are some and here they are:

Turn off – your woman doesn't turn you on any more. Why is that? I am sure many of you haven't even bothered to ask yourself this important question. Meanwhile, you are having less sex, and if this isn't already enough self-punishment, your relationship is also going down the drain. This is just plain stupidity. Have you ever asked yourself how it can be that the woman you once were crazy about, and who made your dick stand at attention the minute she walked into the room, now doesn't interest you sexually?

Over the years you'll experience ups and downs in a relationship, and ideally mastering these relationship cycles will lead to a stronger bond between you and your woman. However, very often couples struggle to emerge as a stronger unit from a downturn cycle. The reason for this, my fellow chaps, is indifference. Indifference is a sneaky and vicious relationship killer. It will not ruin a good relationship overnight, but if you let it into your home and let it nest there, it will grow and grow until at some point you simply give up caring about the important issues in your relationship. Indifference inverts our feelings and disrupts all communication channels. If you have read up to this page, you will know that fucking is also communication and that communication is the oxygen of your relationship; and what happens to any living organism without oxygen? It dies! Before a relationship reaches this terminal condition, it first moves to a state of vegetation, in which you and your woman just live side by side, growing apart from each other with every additional day gone by. What a waste!

Get a grip on yourself and change it today! If you once were passionate about being with your woman, then there is still hope. You should fight to rekindle the passion you once felt for her. Possibly some of the tips and tricks in this book will give you the tools to do just that. Don't get me wrong – even the horniest among us men occasionally are not in the mood for sex, but don't let this evolve into a pattern that could gather momentum and snowball into something serious. Don't let indifference rule your world!

But what if your woman never did turn you on? What?! How can you choose to be with a woman that doesn't excite you sexually? Certainly you must have had your reasons to suppress your basic urges and although it might not seem fair to judge your motives, I hate to be the one to tell you that your situation is hopeless. If you are not sexually aroused by your woman you will try to avoid situations that could trigger sex and you will constantly come up with excuses to keep from fucking your woman. What you are now doing is hurting your woman and she doesn't deserve that.

By nature, we men are better trained and more experienced in dealing with sexual rejection. Throughout our adolescence, and over the course of our entire manhood, all of us men have been turned down by the women we dated, and for certain by the women in our relationships, including our current woman. Women, on the other hand, rarely encounter male opposition when it comes to handing out blow jobs or access to their pussy. A situation where a woman that is wanting to fuck and is turned down by her man raises unpleasant questions. We men are supposed to always be horny and never turn down a free fuck, so there better be a good reason to explain this worrisome and contradictory behavior, and you better be ready to explain to your woman your indisposition to fuck her.

Unfortunately most men are not in sync with their emotions and try to brush them off instead of facing them head on, but it's important to dig up the truth for your incapacity to perform and if possible to overcome the problem and return you to your "regular" self in terms of omnipresent male horniness.

Stress – stress can kill everything, and it will certainly kill your sex life before it kills you. We have all heard this, and especially as we hit the age mark of 40+ we should be smuch more aware of a dangerous build up of stress levels. If you haven't learned how to master and reduce stress levels, it is about time you did. The purpose of this book is not to teach you how to dissolve stress, but to make you aware of it and point out that it can negatively affect your sex life. So whether you choose sports or yoga or meditation or long walks, you need to do something to reduce the stress in your life. If you do it regularly, it becomes a preventative measure that keeps stress from reaching unhealthy and sex-destroying levels. Don't let stress get you down, and certainly don't let it keep your dick down. The paradox is that fucking is an excellent remedy against stress.

While this chapter is primarily about men and the disturbing idea of men reverting to sexcuses for not fucking their women, it needs to also be said here that some forms of stress are more likely to be associated only with women, and we men need to be aware of them. Mostly they revolve around the family – kids and close relatives (especially parents or siblings). The contemporary woman has to wear many hats and she has to be able to multitask with ease. She has to be a housewife, a mother, a friend, a daughter, a co-worker or boss, and of course a lover and a whore. No wonder women are often described as superwomen. Handling all these occupations at once can easily get even the strongest woman stressed out, and we men need to be sensitive about this issue. It is in your best interest to find ways to help your woman with the daily workload, such as doing more work around the house or spending more time with your kids. Look at it this way: anything you take off her plate gives her the time and space to attend to the remaining occupations she has to fulfill, which means that the whore might get a chance to shine this evening.

Apply stress reducing measures to get your woman in the mood, a massage will do wonders (and it doesn't have to be a professional massage) with oil, candlelight and MTFB (music to fuck by). A simple foot massage or neck massage will often work wonders and help to ease the tension and reduce stress levels. Of course if you're in the mood, you can go for the full luxury package. Or prepare a romantic candlelight bath for your woman or offer to join her in the shower; just make sure the water is not too hot, so she will not fall asleep before the action begins. Offer her something to smoke (the occasional joint can work wonders). Cook a nice meal for her and open a good bottle of wine. When you sit down, be empathetic and ask her what's stressing her out. Listen to her and let her spill everything that's on her mind. For women, it is as much about your gesture and good intent, as it is about the soothing effect of your applied actions.

Depression – well, I'm not a shrink, but it goes without saying that if you're in a depressed mood your sexual appetite is severely affected and it can reach a point where it simply doesn't exist anymore. Of course there are various levels of depression, and not every level needs to be cured by popping happy pills. The first thing you need to do is to accept that you have a problem and find the root cause. If you cannot assess it on your own, or are dealing with a chemical imbalance that fucks up your mind, you should seek out professional help. If you experience a long period of sexual abstinence and you are just too tired or not interested at all in fucking your woman, then you may well be dealing with depression.

Don't be ashamed if you decide to see a shrink, and don't be ashamed if you have to take anti-depressants for a while. The positive thing is that once you are on a drug treatment you will notice that your sexual appetite returns, and the more you fuck the better your mental health gets. Again, sport or exercise is a good natural antidepressant, and you are well advised to exercise regularly to improve your mental strength to fight off your depression. Men with a steady sport or fitness routine have a healthier appetite for sex, and that's a fact.

Most importantly, be candid with your woman and don't keep her in the dark about your condition. She needs to know what's messing with your head (or dick), and as much as it may be difficult for her to understand what you are going through, it is the right thing to do to keep your relationship from deteriorating. Don't let your woman misinterpret the situation; defuse any misinterpretations by sharing the truth with her. So here is my own antidepressant cocktail: sex (lots of it), sport or exercise (regularly) and healthy cuisine (no junk food please). Try to get off the pills as quickly as possible and know that the more open you are with your shrink, the better he can understand you, fix you, and set your mind straight.

Impotence – if it's not a medical condition, then it is caused by a mental dysfunction. By the way, most impotency cases are head cases, so there's a good chance you'll overcome it. Same thing here... if you can't get it up over a period of time, don't wait for too long to take on the problem and seek out professional help. The faster you realize you have a problem and are willing to work on it, the better it is for you (and your woman). Typically a man will fall into a depressive mode once he realizes his dick is out of order, and as you can imagine, it only worsens the problem. Impotency is a hard pill to swallow and it hurts us on the deepest personal level, making us feel worthless as men. Getting your cock up whenever you need to is the most basic functionality for a man, and it's the one thing that defines and sets us apart from our female counterparts. As much as it is hurtful to admit that you have a problem with your dick, don't let it ruin your life; stand up and face the problem. Let your woman know that it is you who has a problem and never, ever make the mistake of letting her believe for a second that it is her fault. Don't let her think that you're not able to perform because you're not attracted to her. Honesty is the key to resolving the problem as fast as possible, and a heartfelt talk will clear the air. With a caring and understanding woman at your side, your impotency problem can dissolve much faster than you think.

Once men reach a certain age, we face another problem, but luckily for us, pharmaceutical solutions are available to cure our temporary slackness and assist our dicks in rising as hard as ever. If the time comes to use these wonder pills so you can perform, your duty is to use them. Make sure you consult with your physician first and get a physical to ensure you have a clean bill of health that allows you to engage in extended fuck sessions. Whatever you do, don't choose to pursue illegal channels to get your drugs. Know for sure that your woman would rather have you fucking her less and standing healthy at her side than enjoying a long-lasting fuck fueled by illegal drugs that could cause a potentially disastrous outcome, including a heart attack.

Lastly, I would like to assure you that most men, and this includes your closest friends and relatives, have, at some point in their sexual lifespan, been faced with a temporary incapacity to get their dick up. Most of the time it is nothing to be alarmed about; one-time or rare non-erection experiences happen for various reasons, including stress, tiredness, the influence of drugs, performance anxiety, over-stimulation, or intimidation (caused by beautiful women you believe are out of your league or women you desire just a little too much). A tip I can give you is to think of something entirely different, like work or a good movie, for example (not porn of course). You have to reboot your mind and distance yourself from the current situation, so you can reset your sexual booster. Performance anxiety is something you can control, and mastering it is key to achieving sexual satisfaction – for you and your woman. Then again, if you are unable to control your feelings and thoughts, they will definitely get in the way of your dick and you are likely to lose this battle. The best tactic now is to ask for a rain check. Know that at this point, the more you force it, the smaller your chance is of getting it up again. Any one of the described reasons can lead to a sexual mishap, which denies you the opportunity to show off your sexual prowess and might lead to wrong female conclusions. Know that what could be misconstrued by your woman as impotence can easily be defused through honest communication. And never make the mistake of letting your woman think for a second that you are not getting it up because of her. Be man enough to admit your temporary malfunction. You deserve a second chance and being honest is likely to grant you just that.

Homosexuality – Are you gay? If a naked female ass

or pair of round firm tits doesn't get your dick to rise in sec-onds, and if this is going on for an extended period of time, then there just might be reason for you to dig deep down in your soul to find out if you are not favoring the male gender. It might be one of the toughest things you'll ever have to do in your life, but admitting that you are gay and sharing your enlightening conclusion with your woman is the only fair thing to do. You shouldn't carry on living a lie and hurting everyone around you, including yourself. Yes, admitting you are gay will break up the relationship with your woman and if you have kids it will further complicate things, but you owe it to yourself and certainly to your woman to be honest about your sexual preference. There's a proverb that describes it perfectly: "It's better to make a painful break than draw out the agony."

Of course this goes both ways and it's always possible that your woman could one day come to the conclusion that she fancies the female touch. Still, I honestly believe that many women become lesbians because their men are not enough in tune with their feminine side (i.e., being able to understand and appreciate to some extent how a woman sees the world) and are not able to satisfy a woman's sexual needs. The woman who becomes a lesbian might have had too many unfulfilling sexual experiences and may truly believe that only a woman can satisfy a woman. On the other hand, a woman that loves to be fucked by her man, because he really knows how to satisfy her, will not look out for a woman to replace him. In short, pay attention if you're having a problem, and don't ignore it.

Being honest with yourself and with your woman is pivotal to your happiness, sexual freedom and mental health.

SHRINK IT

What I am going to discuss in this chapter might be disturbing for some of you, but so is the truth. The truth has many faces: it can be liberating, enlightening, joyful, hurting, or frightening – just to name a few possibilities. Many couples are clever enough to realize that they have a severe relationship problem, but instead of facing the hard truth of their failed sexual relationship and working on the actual underlying problem – which is the root cause of their entire crumbling world – they look for the "talking cure." In other words, they seek help from a shrink to help them solve their problems.

Of course, in some cases, shrinks are good; they can highlight problems caused by a couple's miscommunication and act as an unbiased channel for airing frustrations. But that said, I claim that all your time and money is wasted trying to salvage your relationship if you don't enjoy fucking each other. The fact is, if you and your woman enjoy fucking each other, or did until recently, then you have a good chance of saving your relationship. Everything can be fixed if the sex between you is still good (the better the sex is, the better your chances of recovery). However, if the sex you are experiencing is miserable to at least one of you (remember it has to be win-win), then there is little or no hope for a passionate recovery path. Some couples have long ago given up and lost hope of a sexually satisfying relationship. They have settled into an agnostic mode, possibly decided to be content with a platonic relationship, and most likely work hard to suppress their real feelings in order to keep a dysfunctional relationship alive for the wrong reasons.

Then again, some relationships are doomed from day one because sexual compatibility never really existed. Why get serious with a partner if you know that the sex is terrible? Common sense demands that you not buy the car if the engine doesn't start, right? If you are a great mechanic who knows exactly what to do to get the engine running again, yeah – that's a different story, but then again, you always take a car for a test drive. Afterwards you know if it is within your ability to tune the car and transform it into a smooth ride. I still don't understand why many people ignore these signs and are ready to buy a car that clearly isn't going to get the job done.

Finances, kids, and friendship are a few of the reasons that couples cite in order to justify staying in a bad or gone-bad relationship. Yes, they sound like good excuses to stay together, but deep down you already know that there is nothing you can do to erase the feelings of unsatisfied sexual desire. Inevitably the lack of good and mutually satisfying sex will grow into a severe problem. Think hard and ask yourself the tough questions, and I think you will agree with me: if the sex is good, everything else can be fixed. Good fucking between couples improves the trust level and respect for each other, and most importantly, if you are fucking passionately you are communicating on the deepest level without the need to utter a single word.

So back to my original premise, you will seek in vain to reach this form of open and profound communication with the help of a shrink. Deep down you already know the answer to the difficult question of whether or not you have a chance of rescuing your relationship. Without good sex, it simply isn't going to happen.

Therefore, I urge you, all my fellow men, please make it your top priority to learn how to fuck your woman right. It will either improve or save your relationship. I promise you that many of your relationship problems will dissolve if you take my advice to heart and learn more about the female way of thinking and the way women desire to be fucked.

Enough said. My woman just walked in wearing nothing but a thong, and I feel my dick rising to the occasion, which makes it hard to concentrate. So instead of wasting more time writing on this subject (since if you haven't understood it by now you never will), I'm going to attend to her (and my) needs.

Wishing you a fucking good life, Yours Larry

About the Author

Having lived in South Africa, Germany, and Israel, Larry has a multi-cultural view of life. A Renaissance man at heart, he is passionate about pursuing knowledge across a variety of subjects, including the secrets of great sex. After a fulfilling career as a travel industry entrepreneur, which allowed him to travel the world, and then as a restaurateur, which allowed him to pursue his passion for excellent cuisine, he switched over to the hi-tech industry, where he is a creative marketing executive. Larry lives with his wife and his two sons near Tel Aviv, Israel.